Prepared in cooperation with the
Albany Water, Gas, and Light Commission

Groundwater Conditions and Studies in the Albany Area of Dougherty County, Georgia, 2008

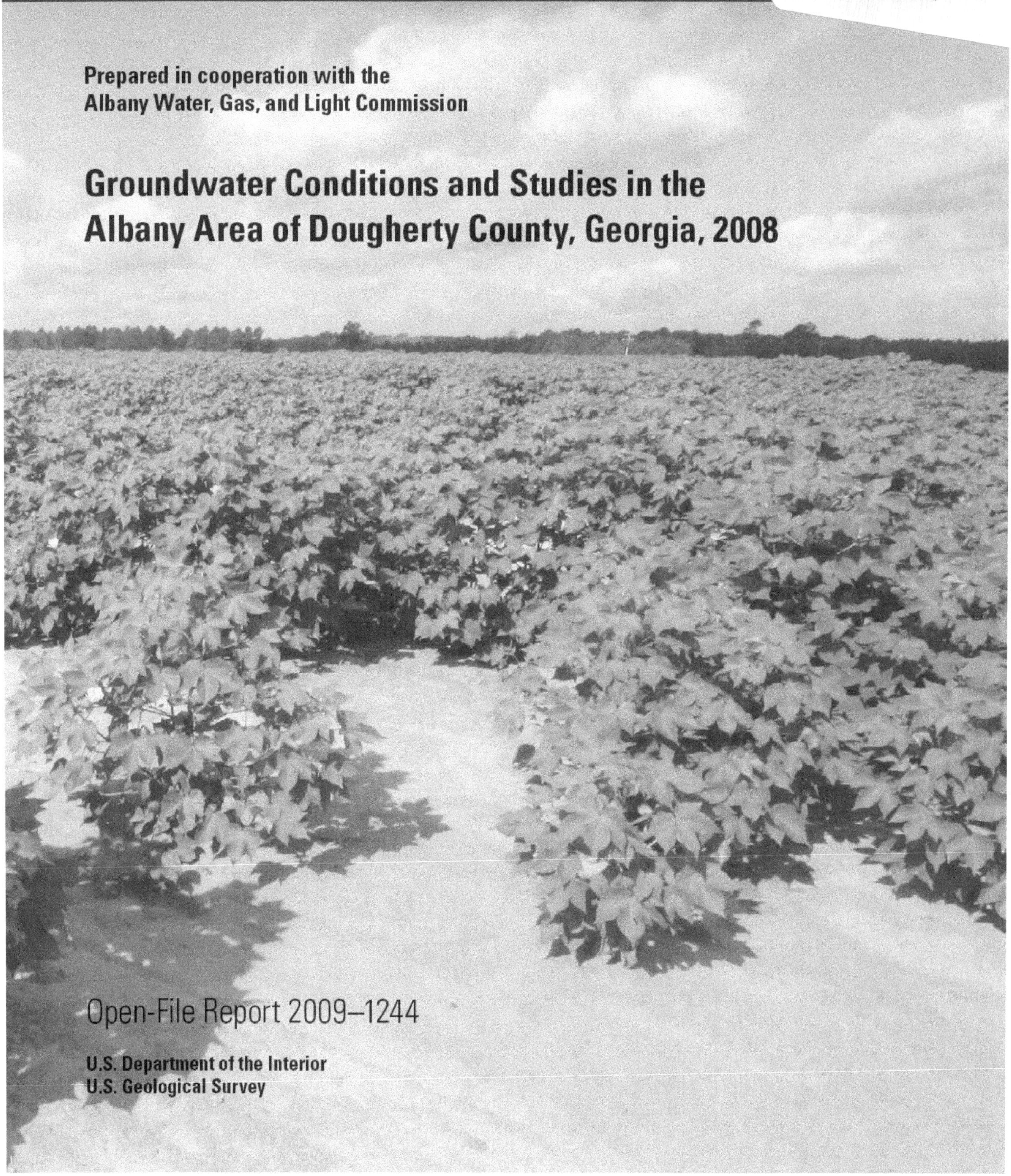

Open-File Report 2009–1244

U.S. Department of the Interior
U.S. Geological Survey

Cover.   Cultivated field of *gossypium* species (cotton), near Bermuda, Dougherty County, Georgia. Photo by Alan M. Cressler, U.S. Geological Survey.

Groundwater Conditions and Studies in the Albany Area of Dougherty County, Georgia, 2008

By Debbie Warner Gordon

Prepared in cooperation with the
    Albany Water, Gas, and Light Commission

Open-File Report 2009–1244

U.S. Department of the Interior
U.S. Geological Survey

U.S. Department of the Interior
KEN SALAZAR, Secretary

U.S. Geological Survey
Suzette M. Kimball, Acting Director

U.S. Geological Survey, Reston, Virginia: 2009

For more information on the USGS—the Federal source for science about the Earth, its natural and living resources, natural hazards, and the environment, visit *http://www.usgs.gov* or call 1-888-ASK-USGS

For an overview of USGS information products, including maps, imagery, and publications, visit *http://www.usgs.gov/pubprod*

To order this and other USGS information products, visit *http://store.usgs.gov*

Suggested citation:
Gordon, D.W., 2009, Groundwater conditions and studies in the Albany area of Dougherty County, Georgia, 2008: U.S. Geological Survey Open-File Report 2009–1244, 54 p.

Contents

Figures

Tables

Conversion Factors and Datums

Multiply	By	To obtain
Length		
inch	2.54	centimeter (cm)
foot (ft)	0.3048	meter (m)
mile (mi)	1.609	kilometer (km)
Flow Rate		
million gallons per day (Mgal/d)	0.04381	cubic meter per second (m^3/s)

Vertical coordinate information is referenced to the North American Vertical Datum of 1988 (NAVD 88), except where indicated otherwise.

Horizontal coordinate information is referenced to the North American Datum of 1983 (NAD 83).

Altitude, as used in this report, refers to distance above the vertical datum.

Specific conductance is given in microsiemens per centimeter at 25 degrees Celsius (µS/cm at 25 °C).

Concentrations of chemical constituents in water are given in milligrams per liter (mg/L) and in micrograms per liter (µg/L).

Acknowledgments

The author appreciates the technical feedback, guidance, and data provided by staff of the Albany Water, Gas, and Light Commission, including Keith Goodin, Lee Daniel, Gary Morfield, and Jim Stolze.

Several U.S. Geological Survey employees assisted in this project. Appreciation is extended to Dorothy F. Payne for consultation and advice during groundwater model development and to Jaime A. Painter for Geographic Information System applications.

Groundwater Conditions and Studies in the Albany Area of Dougherty County, Georgia, 2008

By Debbie Warner Gordon

Abstract

The U.S. Geological Survey has been working cooperatively with the Albany Water, Gas, and Light Commission to monitor groundwater quality and availability since 1977. This report presents an overview of groundwater conditions and studies in the Albany area of Dougherty County, Georgia, during 2008. Historical data also are presented for comparison with 2008 data. Ongoing monitoring activities include continuous water-level recording in 24 wells and periodic water-level measurements in 5 wells. During 2008, water levels in 10 of the continuous-recording wells were below normal, corresponding to lower than average rainfall. Groundwater samples collected from 25 wells in the Upper Floridan aquifer indicate that nitrate levels during 2008 were similar to values from 2007, with a maximum of 12.5 milligrams per liter at one well.

Water samples collected from the Flint River and wells at the Albany well field were analyzed and plotted on a trilinear diagram to show the percent composition of selected major cations and anions. Groundwater constituents (major cations and anions) of the Upper Floridan aquifer at the Albany well field remain distinctly different from those in the water of the Flint River.

To improve the understanding of the groundwater-flow system and nitrate movement in the Upper Floridan aquifer, the U.S. Geological Survey is developing a groundwater-flow model in the Albany area of southwestern Georgia. The model is being calibrated to simulate periods of dry (October 1999) hydrologic conditions. Preliminary results of particle tracking indicate that water flows to the well field from the northwest.

Introduction

Long-term heavy pumping from the Claiborne and Clayton aquifers and the Cretaceous aquifer system (Providence aquifer), which underlie the Upper Floridan aquifer, has resulted in substantial water-level declines in these deep aquifers in the Albany, Georgia, area. To provide additional water supply and reduce the demand on the deep aquifers, the Albany Water, Gas, and Light Commission (WGL) has developed a large well field southwest of Albany (fig. 1). The supply wells at this location are open to the Upper Floridan aquifer, a karstic unit that is the uppermost reliable source of groundwater in the area. Because of local recharge to the aquifer, water quality may be affected by land-use practices. Nitrate levels exceeding the 10-milligrams-per-liter (mg/L) maximum contaminant level (MCL; U.S. Environmental Protection Agency, 2000) have been detected in some wells upgradient from the well field. The complexity of the groundwater-flow system and water quality of the Upper Floridan aquifer near the well field prompted development of a cooperative water program between the U.S. Geological Survey (USGS) and WGL.

Albany Water, Gas, and Light Commission Cooperative Water Program

To address concerns about the quality and availability of groundwater in the Albany area, the USGS and WGL initiated a cooperative water program during 1977. The Federal–State Cooperative Water Program (CWP) is a partnership between the USGS, State, and local agencies that provides information that forms the foundation for many of the Nation's water-resources management and planning activities. The information also may function as an early warning for emerging water problems. The fundamental characteristic of the CWP is that local and State agencies provide at least one-half the funds, and the USGS performs most of the work. The USGS uses consistent techniques to collect and archive data and stores the information in a common database available on the Web. The knowledge gained in the studies is published and added to the growing body of information about the hydrology of the area.

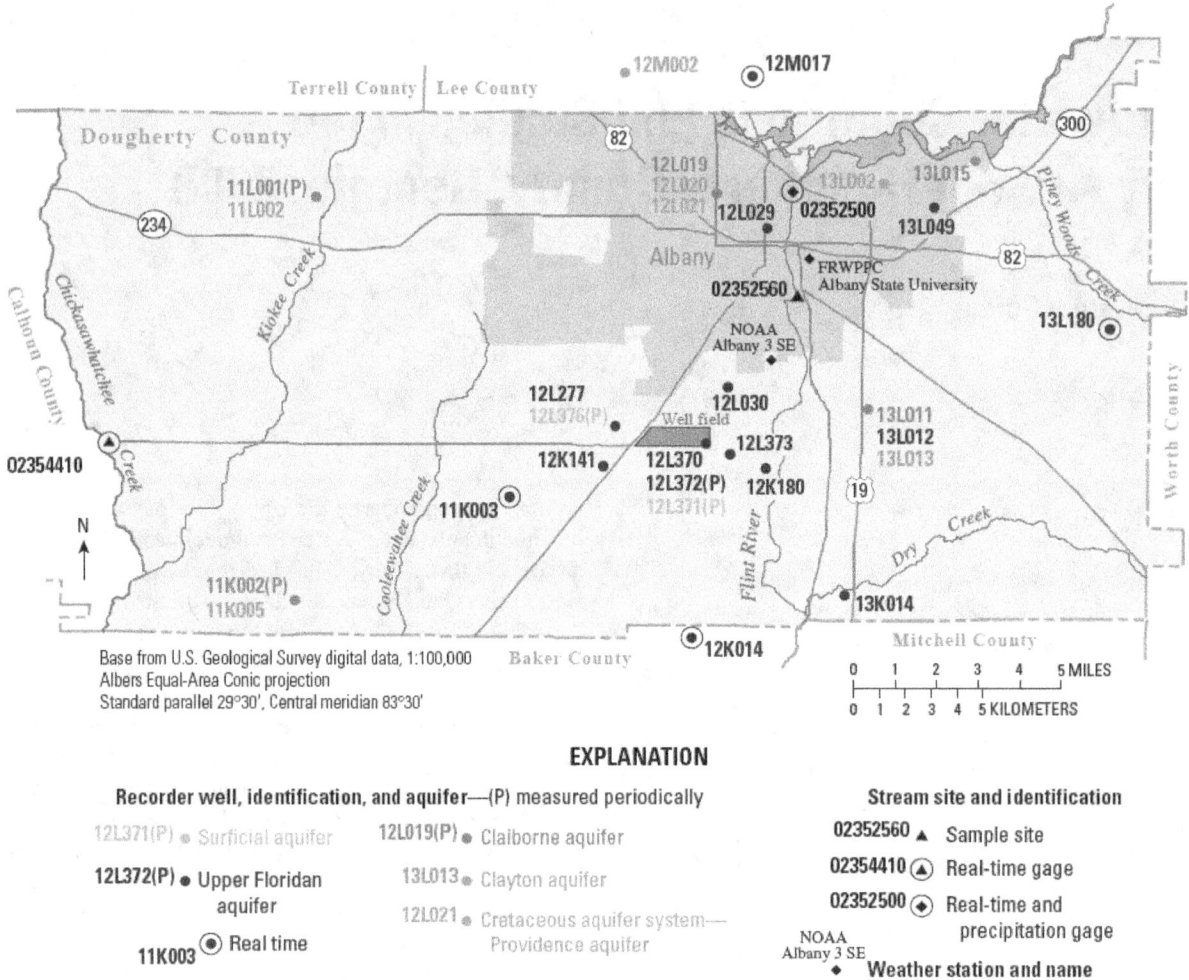

Figure 1.   Monitoring wells and streamgages in the Albany area of Dougherty County, Georgia.

Related Studies

Several studies are currently underway in the southwest Georgia area. In November 2008, groundwater-level data were collected from 376 wells, stream-stage measurements were collected at 111 sites, and stream discharge was measured at 85 sites in the lower Chattahoochee–Flint (CF) and western and central Aucilla–Suwannee–Ochlockonee (ASO) River basins of southwest and south-central Georgia. Because groundwater is the major water source in the basins, and the potential exists for pumping-induced streamflow reduction to affect downstream users, a quantitative understanding of stream-aquifer relations is essential to effectively manage water resources in the lower CF and western and central ASO River basins. The USGS conducted an investigation to document groundwater levels and stream baseflow in the lower CF and western and central ASO River basins during low-flow conditions in November 2008. These data may be used to manage the water supply, to protect water quality, to protect aquatic habitats, by recreational users

(*http://water.usgs.gov/osw/pubs/nhwc_report.pdf*, accessed 08/10/2009), and as a basis for accurate calibration of groundwater-flow models used to simulate water-management scenarios for the region.

The USGS—in cooperation with the State of Georgia Soil and Water Conservation Commission—is conducting a study to evaluate the spatial analysis of annually reported and telemetered water-use data for Georgia. The objectives of the study are to:

- Review existing agricultural water-use data for completeness and consistency;

- Complete descriptive statistics of aggregated data;

- Evaluate how well telemetered water-use data represents the total population of annually reported water-use data; and

- Identify spatial relations between and among telemetered and annually reported water-use sites (L.J. Torak, U.S. Geological Survey, written commun., June 16, 2009).

Purpose and Scope

The objectives of the Albany CWP are to (1) augment the current level of understanding of the hydrogeologic framework of the Upper Floridan aquifer and the occurrence of nitrate contamination near the WGL well field, (2) monitor water-level fluctuations in the four aquifers used in the area and relate water-level trends to changes in climatic conditions and pumping patterns, and (3) evaluate and monitor water quality in the Upper Floridan aquifer as pumping patterns and land-use activities change.

This report provides an overview of groundwater conditions through 2008 and the studies conducted as part of the Albany CWP during 2008. This overview includes a summary of hydrologic conditions based on:

- Continuous water-level monitoring in a 24-well network (fig. 1);

- Construction of a potentiometric-surface map, in the study area, for the Upper Floridan aquifer during November 2008;

- Continuous monitoring of streamflow at the Flint River (02352500, fig. 1) and Chickasawhatchee Creek (02354410), and continuous precipitation monitoring at the Flint River at Albany streamgage (02352500) and Georgia Automated Environmental Monitoring Network site at Albany State University (*http://www.griffin.uga.edu/aemn/cgi-bin/AEMN. pl?site=GAAB* accessed October 9, 2009; Flint River Water, Planning, and Policy Center [FRWPPC] Albany State University);

- Collection of water-quality samples from 25 wells and one site on the Flint River during November 2008, for analysis of dissolved nitrate and major ions and analysis of pesticides at 2 of the wells.

Water-level data for each well for the period of record, nitrate concentrations from 1998 to 2008, precipitation data from 2004 to 2008, and water-use data for every 5 years from 1980 to 2008 are presented for comparison with the 2008 data. In addition to monitoring, the USGS is developing a groundwater-flow model to simulate groundwater flow and nitrate flow paths near the well field. As part of the Albany CWP, water levels are monitored in wells throughout Dougherty County, two wells in Lee County, and one well in Baker County, Georgia (fig. 1).

Well- and Stream-Numbering Systems

In this report, wells are identified using a numbering system based on USGS topographic maps. In Georgia, each 7-1/2-minute topographic quadrangle map has been given a number and letter designation beginning at the southwestern corner of the State. Numbers increase eastward through 39, and letters increase alphabetically northward through "Z" and then become double-letter designations "AA" through "PP." The letters "I" and "O, are not used. Wells inventoried in each quadrangle are numbered sequentially beginning with "1." Thus, the twenty-ninth well inventoried in the Albany West quadrangle (map 12L) is designated 12L029. Springs are considered groundwater sites and are identified in the same manner as wells. Surface-water stations are identified by a numbering system used for all USGS reports and publications since October 1, 1950. The order of listing stations is in a downstream direction along the main channel. All stations on a tributary entering upstream from each mainstream are listed prior to that station. Each surface-water station is assigned a unique 8 - to 14-digit number. Each station number, such as 02352500, begins with the 2-digit identifier "02," which designates it as being a surface-water station, followed by the downstream-order number, "352500," which can range from 6 to 12 digits.

Groundwater Conditions

Groundwater levels in the Albany area of Dougherty County have been monitored for several decades as part of the Albany CWP. Precipitation and groundwater pumpage also are monitored to assess their influence on groundwater conditions. Nitrate concentrations in wells near the Albany well field have been analyzed since the late 1990s. These data are used to guide water-management decisions by State and local authorities.

Factors Influencing Groundwater Levels

Fluctuations and long-term trends in groundwater levels occur as a result of changes in recharge to and discharge from an aquifer. Recharge rates vary in response to precipitation, evapotranspiration, and surface-water infiltration into an aquifer. Discharge occurs as natural flow from an aquifer to streams or springs, as evapotranspiration from shallow water-table aquifers, as leakage to vertically adjacent aquifers, and as withdrawal (pumpage) from wells.

Precipitation

Precipitation in the Albany area of Dougherty County influences groundwater levels in the shallow surficial aquifer system and, to a lesser degree, in the Upper Floridan aquifer. Changes in precipitation also affect quantities of groundwater withdrawn from deeper aquifers and, thus, have an indirect effect on groundwater levels in the Claiborne, Clayton, and Providence aquifers. To monitor precipitation in the Albany area of Dougherty County, a real-time weather station at Albany State University (fig. 1) is operated by the College of Agriculture and Environmental Sciences, University of Georgia, and a real-time streamgage and precipitation site at the Flint River at Albany is operated by the USGS (02352500, fig. 1). Real-time monitoring data for these sites are available at *http://www.griffin.uga.edu/aemn/cgi-bin/ AEMN.pl?site=GAAB* and *http://waterdata.usgs.gov/ga/nwis/ uv/?site_no=02352500&PARAmeter_cd=00045*, respectively (accessed May 15, 2009). Precipitation data also are available for the Albany, Georgia, area from the National Oceanic and Atmospheric Administration (NOAA Albany 3 SE, fig. 1) at *http://cdo.ncdc.noaa.gov/climatenormals/clim84/GA/ GA090140.txt* (accessed May 29, 2009).

Precipitation and cumulative departure from normal data for 2004 through 2008 (NOAA's Albany 3 SE climatic station) are shown in figure 2. The cumulative departure from normal precipitation data can be used to evaluate trends in precipitation that typically relate to recharge of shallow aquifers. Cumulative departure from normal precipitation data describe the long-term surplus or deficit of precipitation during a designated period and are derived by adding successive daily values of departures from normal precipitation data. In this report, daily precipitation data in inches and 30-year (dynamic) normals from NOAA's Albany 3 SE climatic station were used to calculate the cumulative departure from normal (data obtained from *http://cdo.ncdc.noaa.gov/climatenormals/ clim84/GA/GA090140.txt*, accessed May 29, 2009). Normal precipitation for Albany 3 SE is defined as the daily mean values from 1971–2000. A positive cumulative rainfall slope indicates above average rainfall, while a negative slope indicates below average rainfall (*http://cdo.ncdc.noaa.gov/cgi- bin/climatenormals/climatenormals.pl*, accessed July 24, 2009). Cumulative departure data indicate below-normal rainfall through much of 2007 and the first half of 2008.

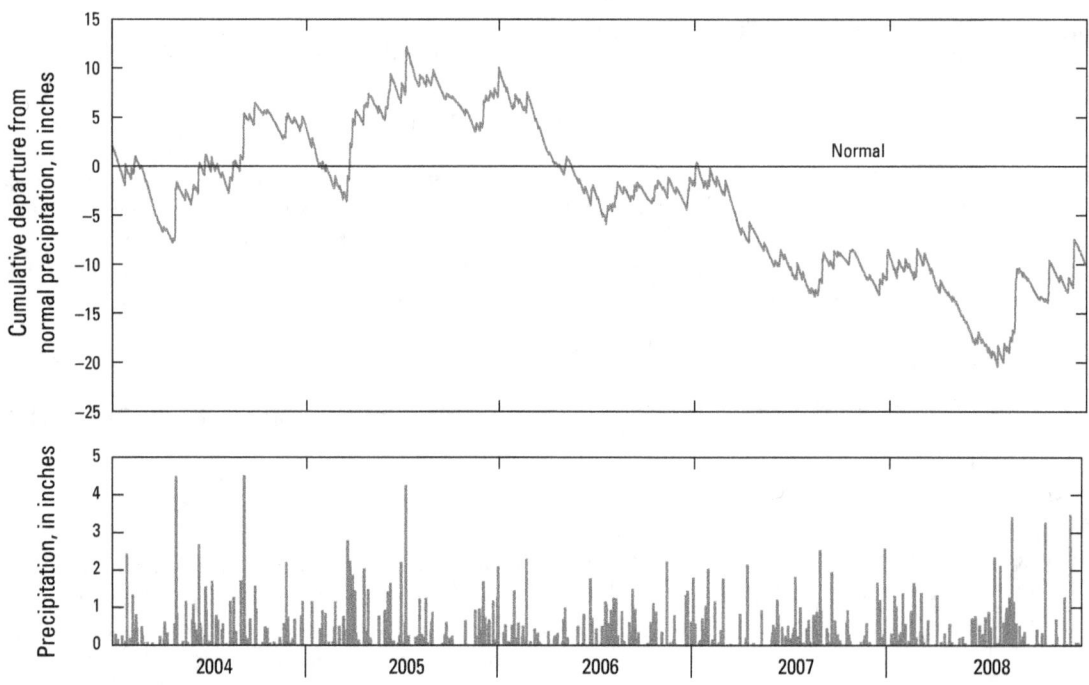

Figure 2. Total daily precipitation data and cumulative departure from normal for January 1, 2004, through December 31, 2008 (NOAA site Albany 3 SE; see fig. 1 for location).

Groundwater Pumpage

Locations of groundwater pumping centers and amounts of water withdrawn from these centers may greatly affect groundwater levels in the Albany area of Dougherty County. Changes in pumping rates and the addition of new pumping centers may alter the configuration of potentiometric surfaces, reverse groundwater flow directions, and increase seasonal and long-term fluctuations in the aquifers.

During 2008, groundwater withdrawals in Dougherty County (excluding irrigation pumping), were about 22 million gallons per day (Mgal/d), of which about 51 percent (11.3 Mgal/d) was for public supply and about 49 percent (10.7 Mgal/d) was for industry (J.L. Fanning, U.S. Geological Survey, written commun., May 27, 2009).

From 2007 to 2008, total withdrawal decreased by 5.3 Mgal/d due largely to the closure of a pharmaceutical company, which accounted for 3.4 Mgal/d of the withdrawal, and a 1.43-Mgal/d reduction in public-supply withdrawals. Irrigation pumping in Dougherty County increased from about 10.9 Mgal/d during 1995 to 20.3 Mgal/d during 2000, then decreased to about 10 Mgal/d during 2005 (fig. 3; Fanning and Trent, 2009). Irrigation-pumping data are not yet available for 2008. The increase in irrigation pumping in 2000 reflects drought conditions that lasted from 1998 until late 2002 (Fanning and Trent, 2009).

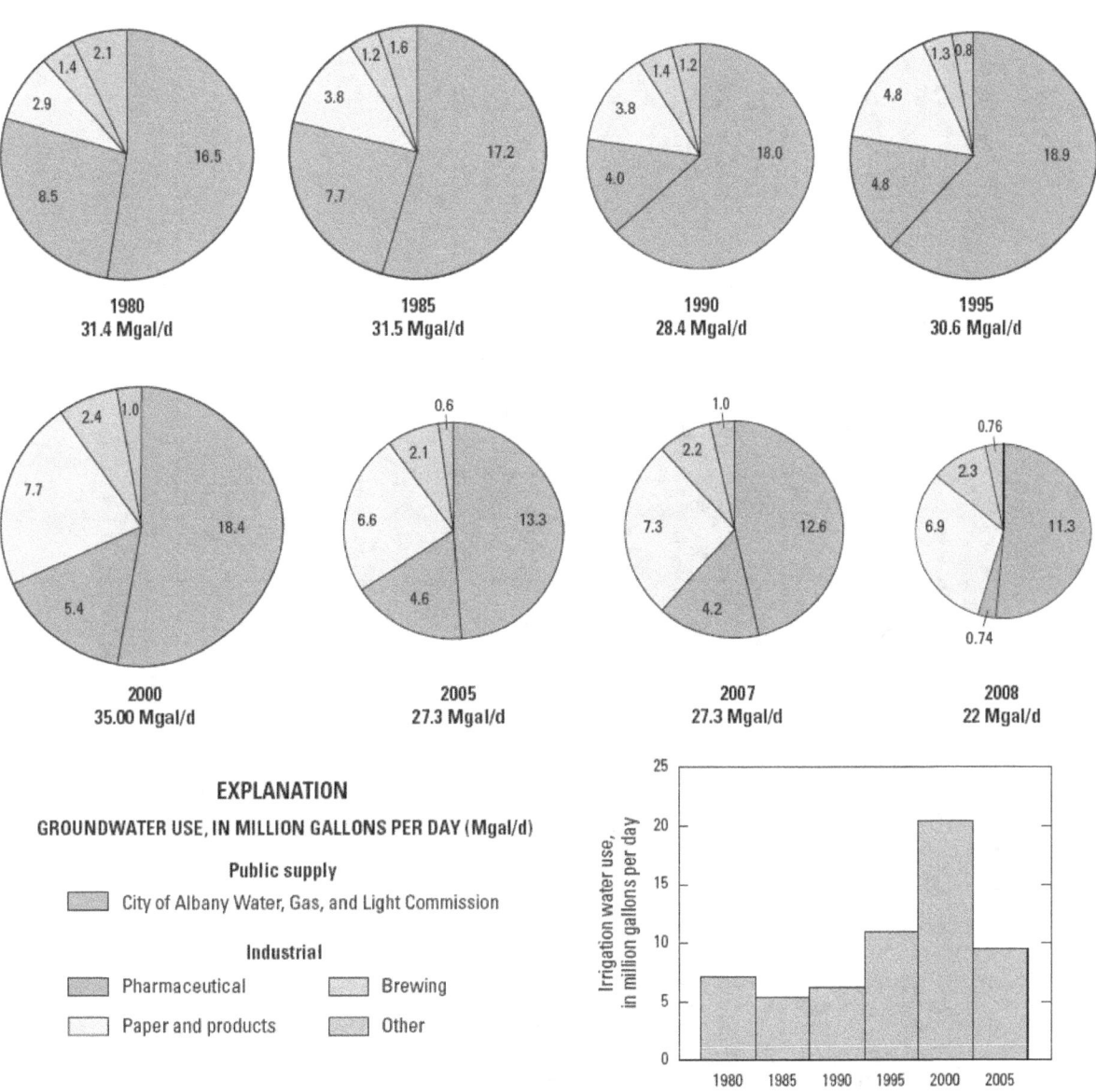

Figure 3. Water-use data from 1980 through 2007. Irrigation data for 2007 and 2008 are not yet available.

Streamflow

Streamflow is monitored in real time on the Flint River at Albany, Georgia (02352500) and Chickasawhatchee Creek near Leary, Georgia (02354410; fig. 1). The gage at the Flint River at Albany was installed in 1901, and the gage at Chickasawhatchee Creek near Leary was installed during May 2001; however, the stage has been measured since 1954. Data for each site are available at *http://waterdata.usgs.gov/ga/nwis/rt*, (accessed May 29, 2009). Daily mean gage height at the Flint River at Albany was below the historical median daily gage height for most of 2008 (fig. 4). The stream stage exceeded the historical median daily gage height periodically during 2008 storms. Daily mean gage height at Chickasawhatchee Creek was close to or slightly greater than the historical median daily gage height from January to about May when stream levels fell below the historical median (fig. 5). In August, stream stage exceeded the historical median periodically during 2008 storms. The relatively low gage height at both sites corresponds to a period of below-normal precipitation that began in 2006 and continued into 2008 (fig. 2).

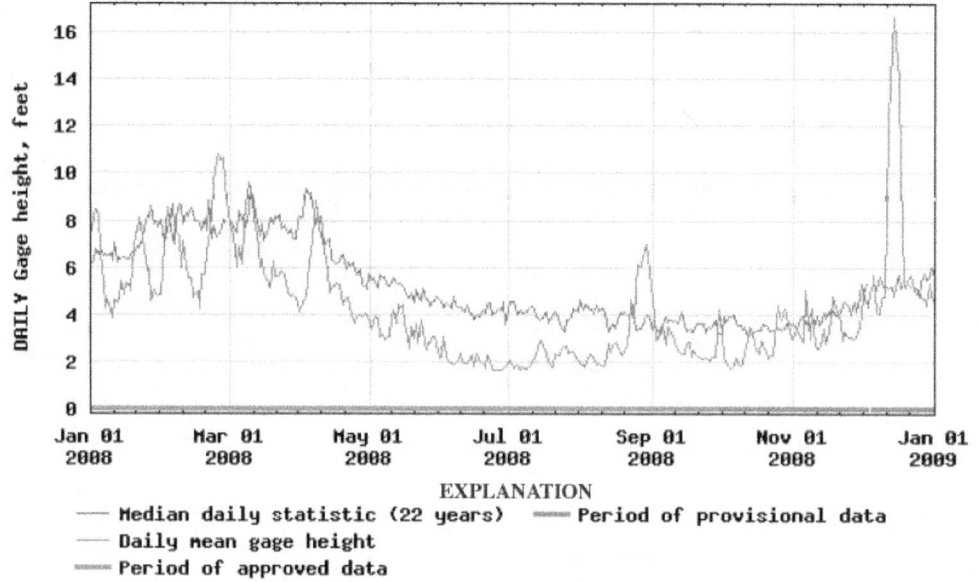

Figure 4.   Daily mean gage height for the Flint River at Albany, Georgia (02352500), 2008. (See fig. 1 for location.)

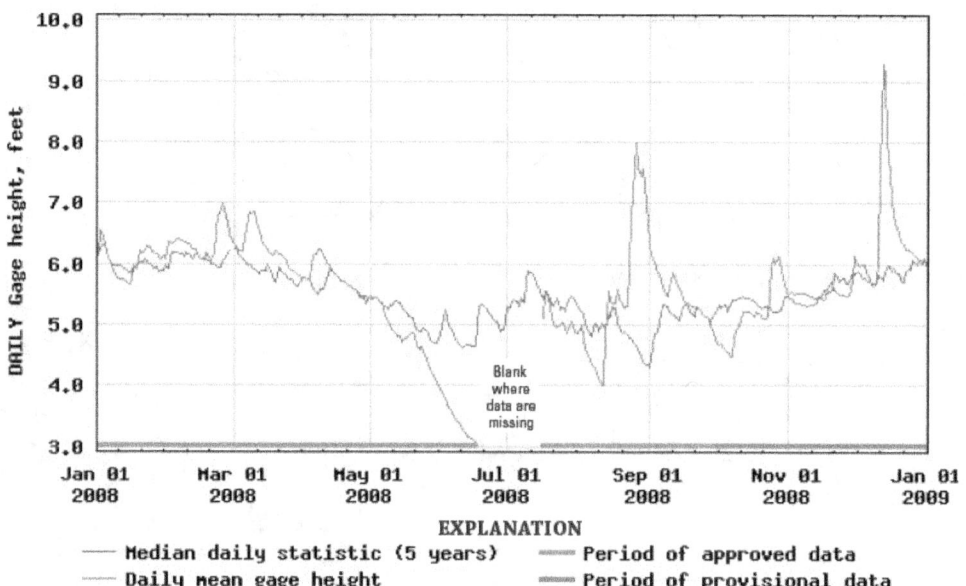

Figure 5.   Daily mean gage height for the Chickasawhatchee Creek near Leary, Georgia (02354410), 2008. (See fig. 1 for location.)

Groundwater Levels

Groundwater levels in the Albany area of Dougherty County are continuously monitored in 14 wells as part of the Albany CWP and in 10 additional wells in conjunction with other projects (fig. 1; table 1). Water levels are measured in another five wells on a periodic basis. All data are available on the Web at *http://waterdata.usgs.gov/ga/nwis/dv?referred_module=gw* (accessed May 15, 2009). Of the 29 wells, 2 are completed in the surficial aquifer, 15 are completed in the Upper Floridan aquifer, 5 are completed in the Claiborne aquifer,

6 are completed in the Clayton aquifer, and 1 is completed in the Providence aquifer (fig. 1, table 1). Hydrographs showing annual daily-mean (2008) water levels and median daily statistics for the period of record for all continuously-monitored wells are presented in Appendix A. Field measurements were added to hydrographs when large periods of data are missing. Hydrographs of water levels measured periodically also are shown in Appendix A. Hydrographs presented in Appendix A and wells listed in table 1 are ordered by aquifer, then sequentially by their site name (well identifier); thus, well 12K141 precedes well 12K180, which precedes well 12L029, and so forth.

Table 1. Recorder wells in the Albany area of Dougherty County, Georgia.

[*, wells measured monthly; project/cooperator: WGL, Water, Gas, and Light Commission; GaEPD, Georgia Environmental Protection Division; FRWPPC, Flint River Water, Planning, and Policy Center]

Well number (fig. 1)	Well name	Aquifer	Project/cooperator	County
12L371*	Albany WGL	Surficial	Albany WGL	Dougherty
12L376*	Albany WGL	Surficial	Albany WGL	Dougherty
11K003	Nilo TW North	Upper Floridan	GaEPD	Dougherty
12K014	Blue Springs OW	Upper Floridan	GaEPD	Baker
12K141	Albany WGL A750 Lower	Upper Floridan	Albany WGL	Dougherty
12K180	EPD MW-2	Upper Floridan	Albany WGL	Dougherty
12L029	USGS TW 13	Upper Floridan	Albany WGL	Dougherty
12L030	USGS TW 16	Upper Floridan	Albany WGL	Dougherty
12L277	Albany WGL	Upper Floridan	Albany WGL	Dougherty
12L370	Albany WGL	Upper Floridan	Albany WGL	Dougherty
12L372*	Albany WGL	Upper Floridan	Albany WGL	Dougherty
12L373	EPD MW-1	Upper Floridan	Albany WGL	Dougherty
12M017	USGS TW 19	Upper Floridan	GaEPD	Lee
13K014	USGS TW 15	Upper Floridan	FRWPPC (Merck & Co., Inc.)	Dougherty
13L012	USGS TW 3	Upper Floridan	Albany WGL	Dougherty
13L049	Turner 1	Upper Floridan	FRWPPC (Miller Brewing Company)	Dougherty
13L180	MCLB Corehole 3 Lower Ocala	Upper Floridan	GaEPD	Dougherty
12L019	USGS TW 5	Claiborne	Albany WGL	Dougherty
13L011	USGS TW 2	Claiborne	Albany WGL	Dougherty
13L015	Turner 2	Claiborne	FRWPPC (Miller Brewing Company)	Dougherty
11K002*	USGS TW 11	Claiborne	Albany WGL	Dougherty
11L001*	USGS TW 4	Claiborne	Albany WGL	Dougherty
11K005	USGS TW 12	Clayton	Albany WGL	Dougherty
11L002	DNR Albany Nursery	Clayton	GaEPD	Dougherty
12L020	USGS TW 6	Clayton	Albany WGL	Dougherty
12M002	USGS TW 9	Clayton	Lee County	Lee
13L002	Albany WGL, Turner City 2	Clayton	GaEPD	Dougherty
13L013	USGS TW 7	Clayton	Albany WGL	Dougherty
12L021	USGS TW 10	Cretaceous aquifer system— Providence aquifer	Albany WGL	Dougherty

Surficial Aquifer

During 2008, water levels were measured six times in well 12L371 and eight times in well 12L376, both of which are completed in the surficial aquifer (table 1; fig. 1). Hydrographs for these wells are presented in Appendix A. Well 12L371 (fig. A–1) was dry when measured in January 2008. The water level rose to about 5 feet above the bottom of the well by March 2008, then again went dry in August, and remained dry through the end of 2008. Well 12L376 (fig. A–2) also was dry when measured in January 2008, but the water level remained above the bottom of the well throughout the rest of 2008.

Upper Floridan Aquifer

Water levels in the Upper Floridan aquifer are monitored in 15 wells (fig. 1). Hydrographs for these wells are presented in Appendix A.

Water levels in the Upper Floridan aquifer generally were below or near the historical median daily values for the first half of 2008, corresponding to below-normal rainfall and increased pumping. While water levels were below historical daily mean for most of 2008, most had risen above historical levels by December 2008. Upper Floridan aquifer water levels in the eastern part of Dougherty County were near the historical median daily values through August 2008. In September water levels rose above the historical median daily values because of large amounts of precipitation (well 13L180; fig. A–17). Water levels fell below historical median values again in October but once again rose above normal in December 2008.

A potentiometric-surface map for the Upper Floridan aquifer was constructed using data from 81 wells in the southwestern Albany area during November 3–10, 2008 (fig. 6). The potentiometric contours are similar to those for 2007; water generally flows from northwest to southeast in the Albany area of Dougherty County, with no evidence of a cone of depression at the well field. Water levels were slightly higher during November 2008 than during the fall of 2007.

Claiborne Aquifer

Water levels are monitored in five wells completed in the Claiborne aquifer (table 1; fig. 1). Hydrographs for these wells are presented in Appendix A.

Water levels in the Claiborne aquifer indicate delayed response to precipitation and a more rapid response to pumping changes than those in the Upper Floridan aquifer. Water levels in well 13L015 (fig. A–20) were generally below the historical median daily values except in August and December 2008. Data for well 13L011 (fig. A–19) are unavailable for much of the first half of 2008 because of equipment malfunction. During the second half of the year, water levels in well 13L011 were above the daily median. The variability between the two wells probably is because of the localized effects of pumping.

Clayton and Providence Aquifers

Water levels are monitored in six wells completed in the Clayton aquifer and in one well completed in the Providence aquifer (table 1, fig. 1). Hydrographs for these wells are presented in Appendix A, figures A–23 through A–29.

Like the Claiborne aquifer, the Clayton and Providence aquifers do not respond quickly to precipitation and are affected mostly by pumping. Water levels in the Clayton aquifer during 2008 were below the historical median daily values in wells 11K005 and 11L002, and above the historical median daily values in well 13L013. Water levels in well 13L002 were near the historical median daily values throughout 2008. Water levels in well 12L020 were available only from January through July 2008, and were above the historical median daily values during that time. Water levels in well 12L021, completed in the Providence aquifer, were above the historical median daily values throughout 2008.

Sinkhole Development

No new sink holes developed at the well field in 2008 (Jim Stolze, Albany Water, Gas, and Light Commission, written commun., December 23, 2008). Figure 7 shows a map of sinkholes that formed on the well field prior to 2008. The large number of sinkholes that developed during 2007 may be a result of low water levels that followed a period of high water levels in 2006 (fig. 8).

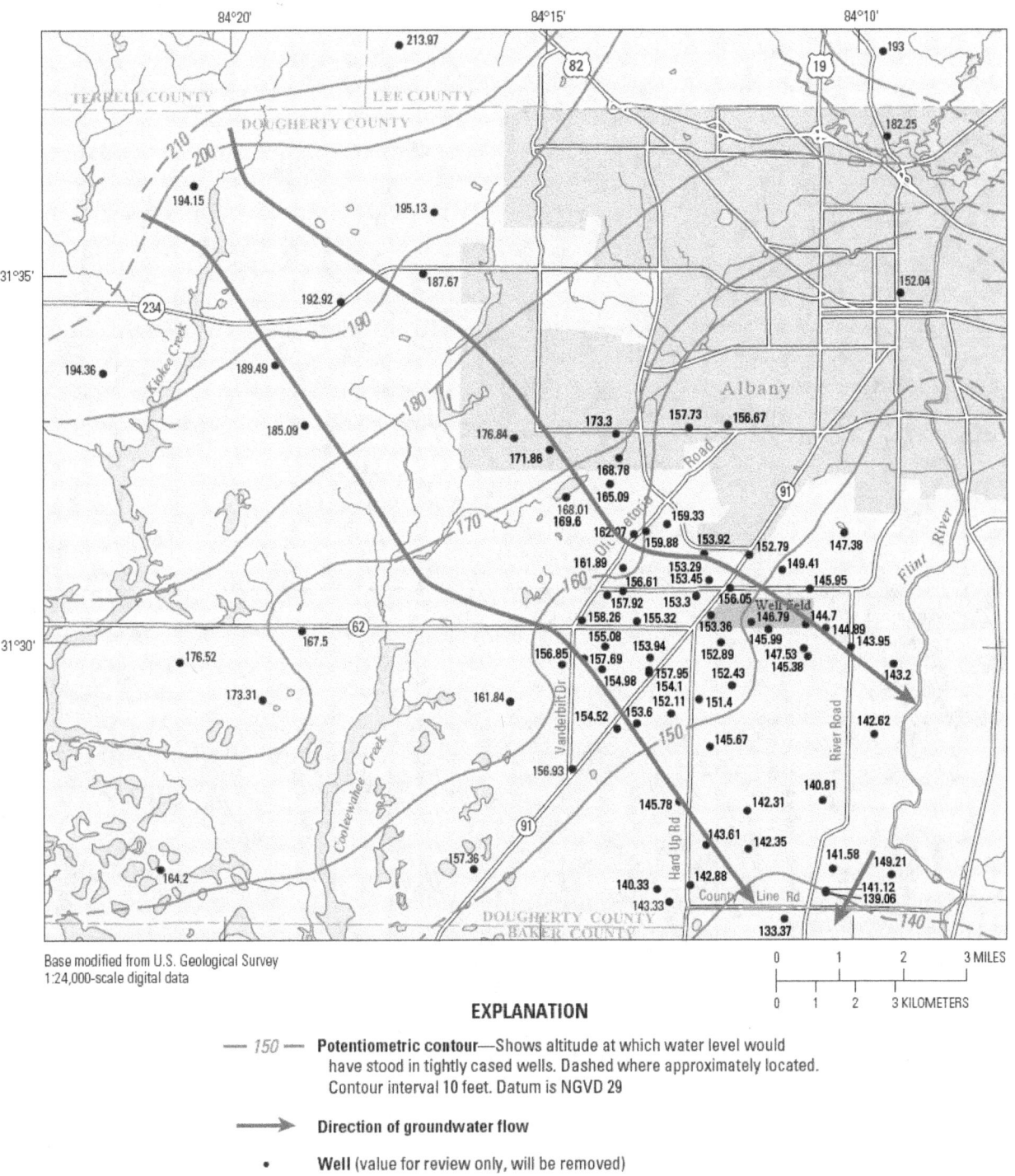

Figure 6. Potentiometric surface of the Upper Floridan aquifer in the Albany area, Dougherty County, Georgia, November 3–10, 2008.

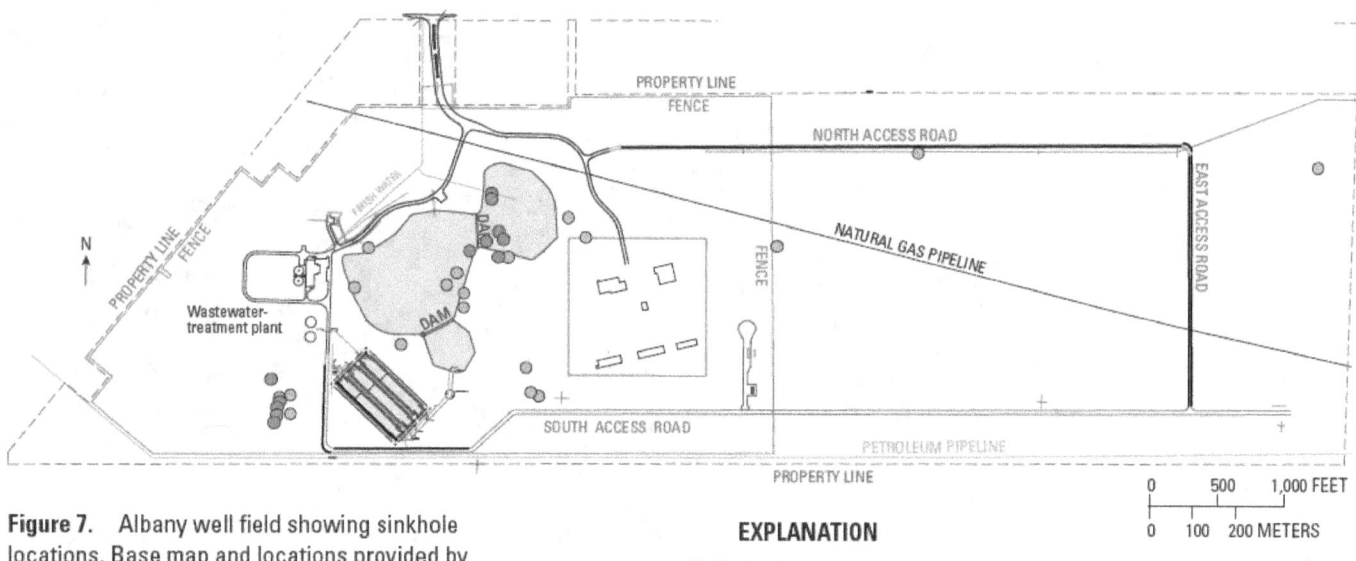

Figure 7. Albany well field showing sinkhole locations. Base map and locations provided by Albany Water, Gas, and Light Commission.

EXPLANATION

Sinkhole—Year developed

◉ Prior to 2007   ● 2007

Figure 8. Water levels in well 12L277 and number of sinkholes that developed in the Albany well field during 2006 through 2008. (See fig. 1 for location.)

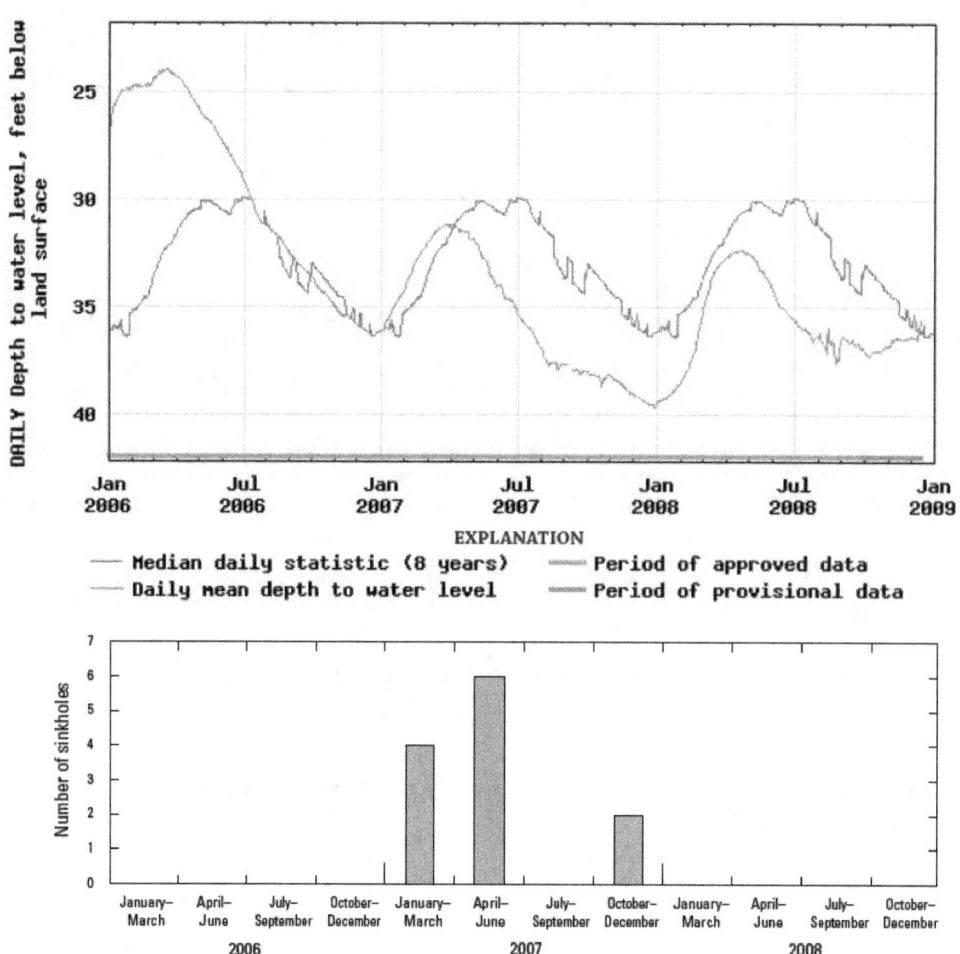

Groundwater Quality of the Upper Floridan Aquifer

Water samples were collected from 25 wells in the southwest area of Albany during November 3–20, 2008 (Appendix B). Of the 25 wells sampled, 14 are located in the well field area where samples have been collected annually for the past 10 years. The samples were analyzed for cations, anions, and nutrients. A sample from well 12L061 completed in the Upper Floridan aquifer had a nitrate plus nitrite concentration of 12.5 mg/L, greater than the 10-mg/L MCL (fig. 9, table 2). Water from well 12L376, completed in the surficial aquifer, had a nitrate plus nitrite concentration of 10.1 mg/L. Since October 2007, nitrate levels have increased in seven wells, decreased in three wells, and remained unchanged in one well (table 2). One well that was measured in 2007 was not measured in 2008.

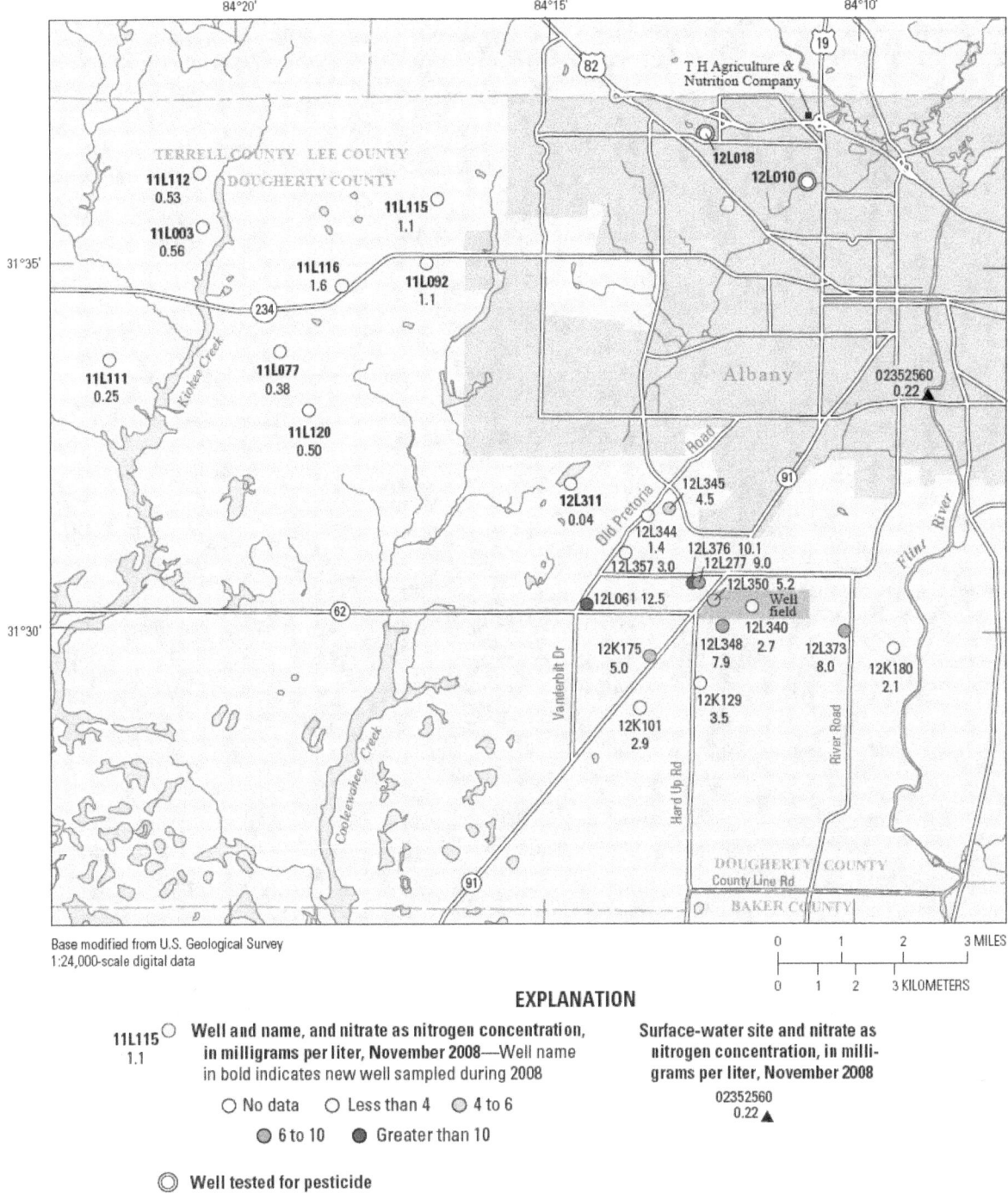

Figure 9.   Nitrate concentrations at selected groundwater and surface water sites in the Albany area, Georgia, November 2008.

Table 2. Nitrate data from selected wells in the Albany area of Dougherty County, Georgia, 1998–2008 (wells are open to the Upper Floridan aquifer, well 12L376 is open to the surficial aquifer, and 2352560 is a gage on the Flint River).

[Sept, September; Nov, November; Oct, October; NO$_3$–N, nitrate as nitrogen; NO$_2$ + NO$_3$ as N, nitrite plus nitrate as nitrogen; —, no data]

Site name (fig. 9)	July 1993 NO2 + NO3 as N	Sept 1998 NO3–N	April 1999 NO3–N	April 2001 NO2 + NO3 as N	Nov 2001 Dissolved NO2 + NO3 as N	Nov 2002 NO3–N	May 2003 NO3–N	Nov 2003 NO3–N	Nov 2004 NO3–N	Nov 2005 NO3–N	Nov 2006 Dissolved NO2 + NO3 as N	Oct 2007 Dissolved NO2 + NO3 as N	Nov 2008 Dissolved NO2 + NO3 as N
					Concentration, in milligrams per liter								
					Wells								
12K053		—	—	—	—	2.0	—	2.2	1.9	2.2	2.2	2.1	—
12K101	—	1.8	1.9	—	2.2	2.1	—	2.1	2.0	2.4	2.6	2.7	2.9
12K129		—	—	—	3.1	2.9	—	2.9	2.8	2.7	3.3	3.3	3.5
12K175	—	3.8	5.7	5.0	5.9	5.4	—	6.1	5.5	7.0	6.2	6.0	5.0
12K180	—	—	—	—	—	1.56	1.7	1.4	1.4	1.7	2.0	2.1	2.1
11L003	0.58	—	—	—	—	—	—	—	—	—	—	—	0.56
11L077	—	—	—	—	—	—	—	—	—	—	—	—	0.38
11L092	1.2	—	—	—	—	—	—	—	—	—	—	—	1.1
11L111	0.23	—	—	—	—	—	—	—	—	—	—	—	0.25
11L112	0.31	—	—	—	—	—	—	—	—	—	—	—	0.53
11L115	—	—	—	—	—	—	—	—	—	—	—	—	1.1
11L116	1.2	—	—	—	—	—	—	—	—	—	—	—	1.6
11L120	—	—	—	—	—	—	—	—	—	—	—	—	0.50
12L010	—	—	—	—	—	—	—	—	—	—	—	—	—
12L018	—	—	—	—	—	—	—	—	—	—	—	—	—
12L061	—	11	12	12	12	12.5	—	13.4	13.1	13.7	12.5	12.3	12.5
12L277	—	7.5	6.9	6.5	8.0	6.3	9.0	8.2	8.4	8.9	8.9	8.9	9.0
12L311	—	—	—	—	—	—	—	—	—	—	—	—	0.04
12L339	—	5.9	5.4	—	5.0	—	—	—	—	6.0	—	—	—
12L340	—	—	—	—	—	—	—	—	4.7	5.0	5.8	3.7	2.7
12L344	—	6.0	5.1	2.7	1.6	1.7	—	1.9	2.1	3.0	—	—	1.4
12L345	—	—	—	—	—	—	—	—	—	—	—	—	4.5
12L346	—	—	—	—	—	—	—	7.2	6.6	8.1	—	—	—
12L348	—	—	6.5	6.4	7.1	6.8	—	6.9	6.6	7.0	7.1	7.4	7.9
12L350	—	3.0	2.9	—	4.8	5.5	—	2.6	2.0	1.8	3.3	2.7	5.2
12L357	—	5.9	3.1	—	2.0	—	—	—	3.5	5.1	3.8	—	3.0
12L370	—	—	—	—	—	—	—	7.1	—	—	—	—	—
12L373	—	—	—	—	7.2	6.6	8.6	7.5	7.2	7.6	7.9	8.3	8.0
12L376	—	—	—	—	—	6.5	8.8	8.3	9.2	11.5	10.9	9.9	10.1
					Surface-water site								
02352560	—	—	—	—	—	—	0.4	0.45	0.41	0.45	0.38	0.26	0.22

Since 1998, nitrate concentrations have increased slightly; however, a few of the wells show a decrease since 2005 (wells 12L061, 12L376, and 12L357; fig. 10, table 2).

To assess nitrate concentrations in an area believed to provide recharge to the Upper Floridan aquifer, samples were collected from nine additional wells northwest of the well field (fig. 9). The recharge area was delineated by preliminary simulations from a groundwater-flow model of the Upper Floridan aquifer (Gordon, 2008). These samples also were analyzed for cations, anions, and nutrients. Nitrate plus nitrite concentrations in the nine wells ranged from 0.04 to 1.6 mg/L (fig. 9; table 2). Five of the nine wells were sampled in July 1993, and nitrite plus nitrate concentrations were similar to those obtained in 2008 (table 2).

A hazardous waste site, the T H Agriculture & Nutrition (THAN) Company Superfund Site, is located in the northern part of Albany (fig. 9). Samples collected in 2007 indicate the 2008 health-based criteria in groundwater were exceeded for 1,2-dibromoethane, aldrin, alpha-BHC (an alpha isomer of benzene hexachloride), beta-BHC (a beta isomer of benzene

hexachloride), 4,4'-dichlorodiphenyltrichloroethane (DDT), dieldrin, toxaphene, and xylene. In May 2008, a 66-foot-deep well contained 20 micrograms per liter (µg/L) of technical toxaphene (U.S. Environmental Protection Agency, written commun., second 5-year review report, September 2008). Sample analysis indicates that toxaphene concentrations have been increasing in downgradient, perimeter, and off-site shallow wells completed in the Upper Floridan aquifer. There also is some evidence of vertical contaminant migration (U.S. Environmental Protection Agency, written commun., second 5-year review report, September 2008). The USGS sampled two of WGL's municipal supply wells for pesticides (wells 12L010 and 12L018; fig. 9). The sample from well 12L010 contained no detectable pesticides, and the sample from well 12L018 had very low concentrations of p,p'-methoxychlor (0.0014 µg/L), which is below the reporting limit and 3 orders of magnitude below the MCL of 0.04 mg/L (U.S. Environmental Protection Agency, 2000; Appendix B). Although such a low concentration is not a cause for concern, continued monitoring could enable tracking of any increasing trend.

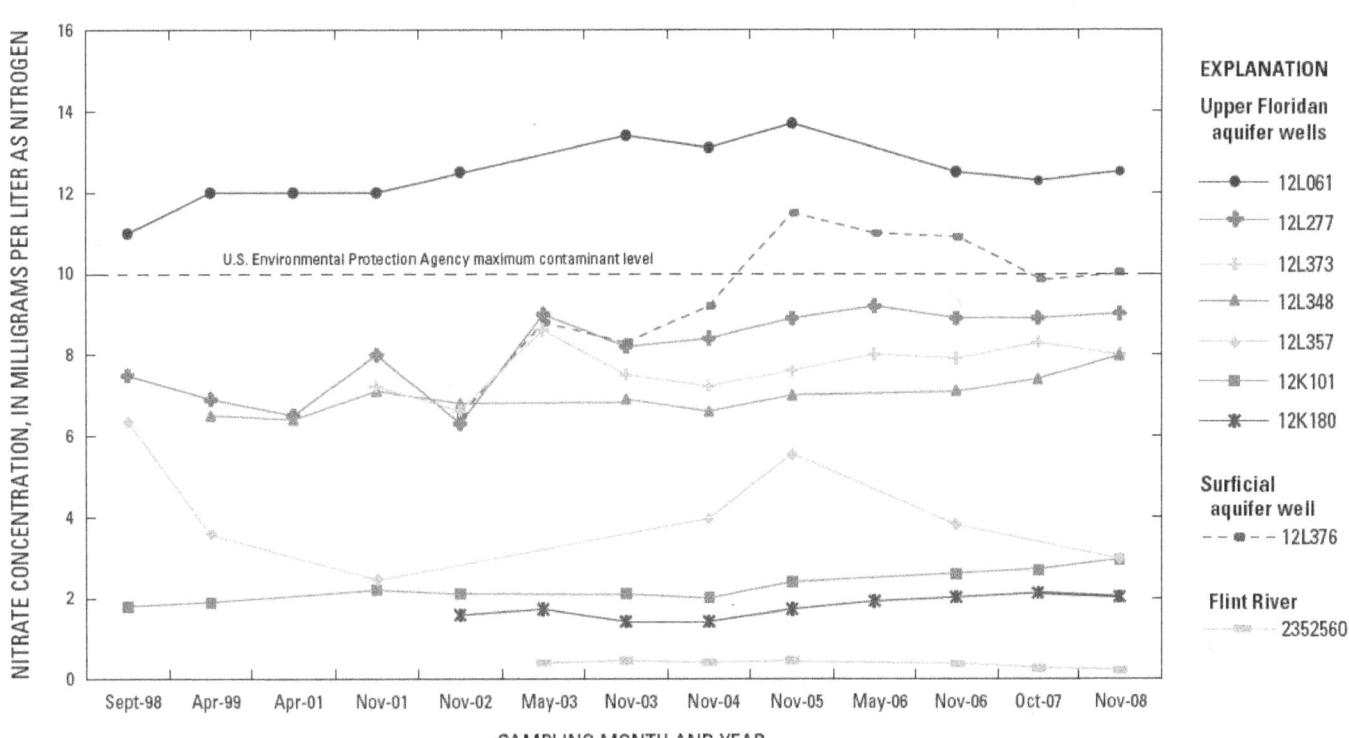

Figure 10. Nitrate concentrations at selected groundwater wells and the Flint River, September 1998– November 2008. (See fig. 9 for locations.)

A surface-water sample was collected from the Flint River at the West Oakridge Drive bridge on November 5, 2008 (02352530, fig. 1) for comparison of the water-quality characteristics of surface and groundwater. A trilinear diagram showing the percent composition of selected major cations and anions is presented in figure 11. This diagram shows that the groundwater quality of the Upper Floridan aquifer remains distinctly different from the water quality of the Flint River, as was the case during 2003–2007 (Gordon, 2008). Water from the Upper Floridan aquifer is supersaturated with calcium, and water from the Flint River contains more of the other constituents such as sodium, potassium, and magnesium.

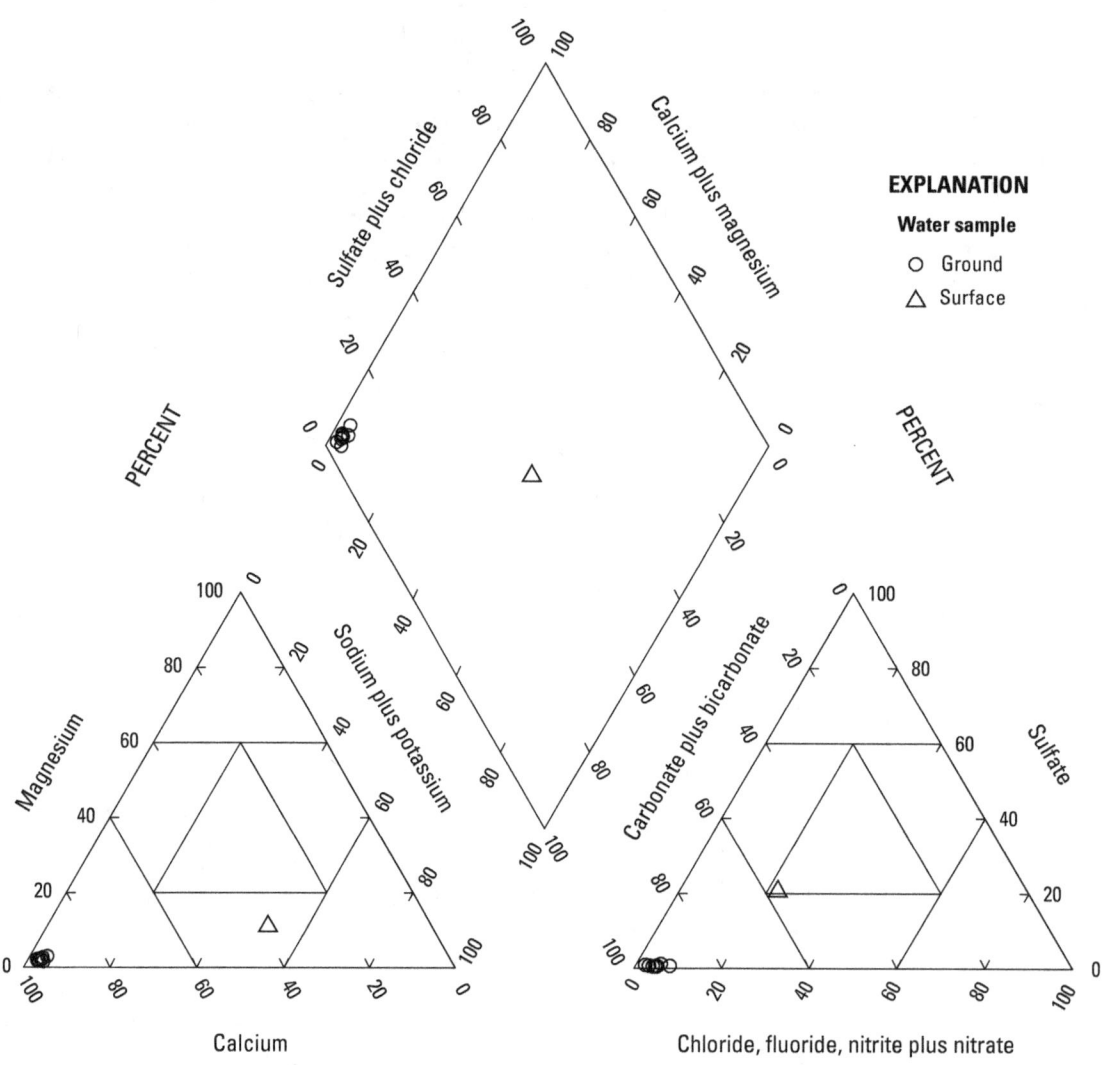

Figure 11.   Trilinear diagram showing water quality of the Upper Floridan aquifer and the Flint River at Albany, Georgia, November 2008.

Groundwater Studies

The Albany CWP provides for the ongoing collection of hydrologic data to provide a better understanding of hydrologic conditions, water quality, and groundwater flow paths in the Albany area of Dougherty County. During 2008, the principal focus of groundwater studies for the Albany CWP was calibrating a groundwater-flow model to simulate flow paths of the Upper Floridan aquifer to the Albany well field. The model was calibrated and flow paths to the well field were simulated (fig. 12). The model indicates that water pumped from the Upper Floridan aquifer at the well field originates northwest of the well field.

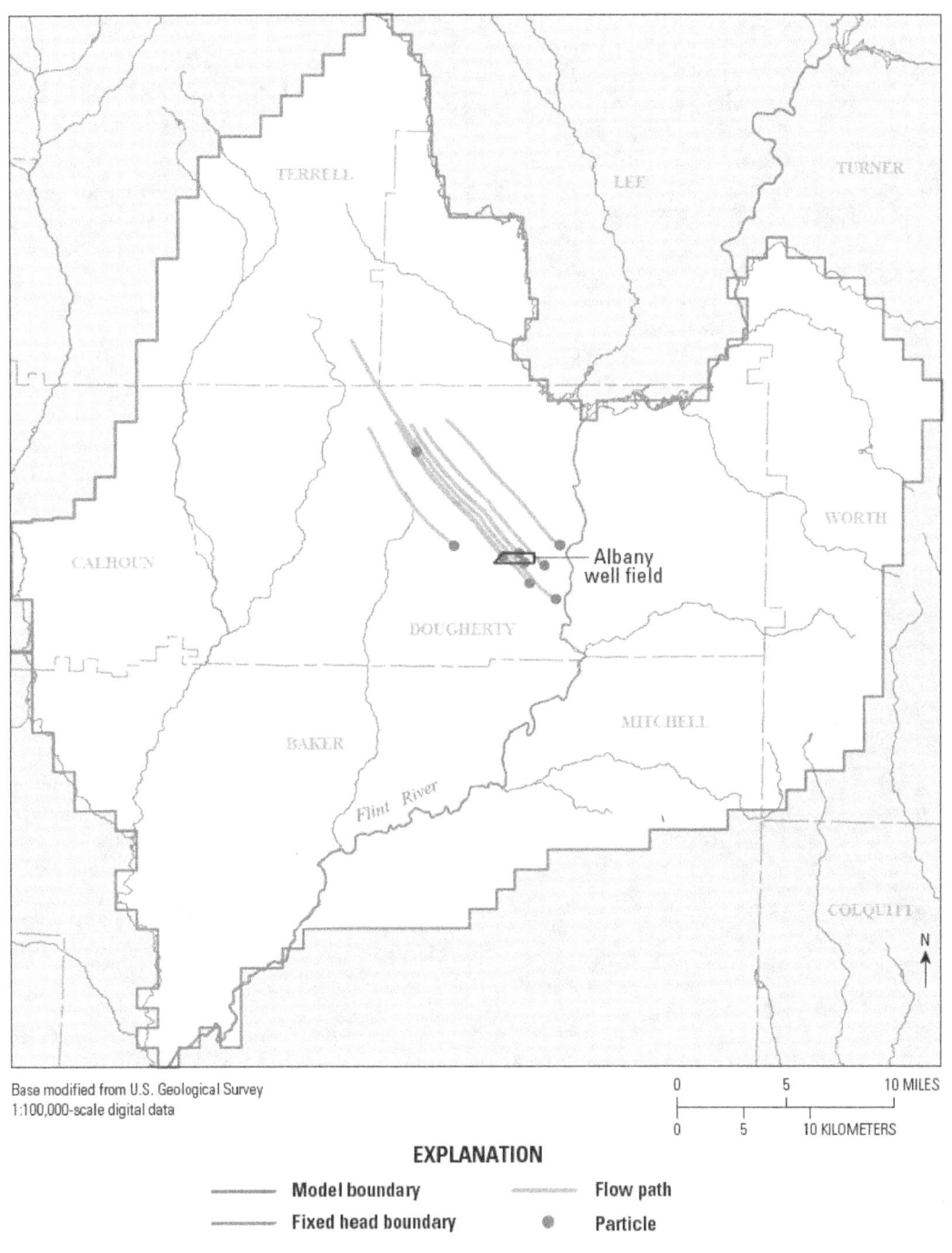

Base modified from U.S. Geological Survey
1:100,000-scale digital data

0   5   10 MILES

0   5   10 KILOMETERS

EXPLANATION

——— Model boundary   ～～～ Flow path

——— Fixed head boundary   ● Particle

Figure 12.   Simulated flow paths from a groundwater-flow model calibrated to October 1999 conditions.

A regional groundwater-flow model that includes the Albany well field area is being developed by the USGS Water Science Center in Tallahassee, Florida (fig. 13). This model has several advanced features not included with the model presently being used in the well field area, including methods used previously in the Transport to Anthropogenic and Natural Contaminants (TANC) study conducted by the USGS National Water-Quality Assessment Program in the Tampa Bay region (Crandall, 2007; Katz and others, 2007; Crandall and others, 2009) to predict recharge areas and travel times for flow paths (Eberts and others, 2005; C.A. Crandall, U.S. Geological Survey, written commun., July 10, 2009). Sinkholes and total drainage area of all depressions within a grid cell were used to create a multiplier array that was combined with regional estimates of hydraulic conductivity for the Upper Floridan aquifer from the models used in studies by Torak and McDowell (1996) and Jones and Torak (2006) to calculate recharge estimates for the regional model (C.A. Crandall, U.S. Geological Survey, written commun., July 10, 2009). When completed, the input hydrologic data and boundary flow data from the calibrated regional model can be used to improve the current Albany well field model.

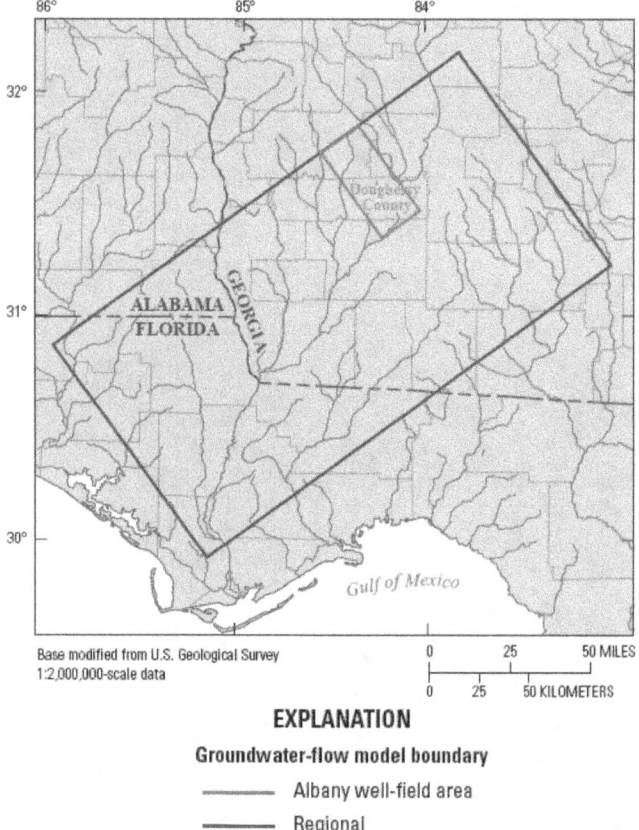

Figure 13.   Location of regional groundwater-flow model and Albany well-field flow model.

Reports and Technical Presentations

The USGS prepared several reports and technical presentations on southwestern Georgia during 2008. Recent reports and presentations include:

- "Georgia's ground-water resources and monitoring network, 2008" (*http://ga.water.usgs.gov/ publications/fs2008-3072/pdf/fs2008-3072.pdf*, accessed May 26, 2009).

- "Ground-water conditions and studies in the Albany area of Dougherty County, Georgia, 2007" (*http://pubs. usgs.gov/of/2008/1328/*, accessed May 26, 2009).

- "Groundwater flow and particle-tracking in the Albany area" presentation at the spring conference of the Georgia Association of Water Professionals, April 2008, and to the Georgia Groundwater Association, July 2008.

Summary

This report provides hydrologic, geologic, and water-quality data needed to manage water resources effectively in the city of Albany and Dougherty County, Georgia. An overview of groundwater conditions through 2008 and studies conducted as part of the Albany Cooperative Water Program during 2008 are presented.

During 2008, water levels in 10 out of 24 continuous-recording wells were below normal, corresponding to lower than average rainfall. Groundwater samples collected from 25 wells in the Upper Floridan aquifer indicate that nitrate levels during 2008 were similar to values from 2007, with a maximum of 12.5 milligrams per liter at well 12L061. Water samples collected from the Flint River and wells at the Albany well field were analyzed and plotted on a trilinear diagram to show the percent composition of selected major cations and anions. Groundwater constituents (major cations and anions) of the Upper Floridan aquifer at the Albany well field remain distinctly different from those in the water of the Flint River.

The USGS is developing a groundwater-flow model in the Albany area of southwestern Georgia to improve the understanding of the groundwater-flow system and nitrate movement in the Upper Floridan aquifer. The model is being calibrated to simulate periods of dry (October 1999) hydrologic conditions. Preliminary results of particle tracking indicate that water flows to the well field from the northwest.

Selected References

Crandall, Christy, 2007, Hydrogeologic setting and ground-water flow simulations of the Northern Tampa Bay regional study area, Florida, *in* Paschke, S.S., ed., Hydrogeologic settings and ground-water flow simulations for regional studies of the transport of anthropogenic and natural contaminants to public-supply wells—Studies begun in 2001: U.S. Geological Survey Professional Paper 1737-A, Section 5; accessed September 3, 2009, at *http://pubs.usgs.gov/pp/2007/1737a/Section5.pdf.*

Crandall, C.A., Kauffman, L.J., Katz, B.G., Metz, P.A., McBride, W.S., and Berndt, M.P., 2009, Simulations of groundwater flow and particle tracking analysis in the area contributing recharge to a public-supply well near Tampa, Florida, 2002–05, U.S. Geological Survey Scientific Investigations Report 2008–5231, 53 p.

Eberts, S.M., Erwin, M.L., and Hamilton, P.A., 2005, Assessing the vulnerability of public-supply wells to contamination from urban, agricultural, and natural sources: U.S. Geological Survey Fact Sheet 2005–3022, 4 p.

Fanning, J.L., and Trent, V.P., 2009, Water Use in Georgia by County for 2005; and Water-Use Trends, 1980–2005: U.S. Geological Survey Scientific Investigations Report 2009–5002, 186 p.; Web-only publication available at *http://pubs.usgs.gov/sir/2009/5002/.*

Gordon, D.W., 2008, Ground-water conditions and studies in the Albany area of Dougherty County, Georgia, 2007: U.S. Geological Survey Open-File Report 2008–1328, 49 p.; Web-only publication available at *http://pubs.usgs.gov/of/2008/1328/.*

Jones, L.E., and Torak, L.J., 2006, Simulated effects of seasonal ground-water pumpage for irrigation on hydrologic conditions in the lower Apalachicola–Chattahoochee–Flint River Basin, southwestern Georgia and parts of Alabama and Florida, 1999–2002: U.S. Geological Survey Scientific Investigations Report 2006–5234, 83 p.; Web-only publication available at *http://pubs.usgs.gov/sir/2006/5234/.*

Katz, B.G., Crandall, C.A., Metz, P.A., McBride, W.S., and Berndt, M.P., 2007, Chemical characteristics, water sources and pathways, and age distribution of ground water in the contributing recharge area of a public-supply well near Tampa, Florida, 2002–05: U.S. Geological Survey Scientific Investigations Report 2007–5139, 85 p.

Peck, M.F., Painter, J.A., and Leeth, D.C., 2009, Ground-water conditions and studies in Georgia, 2006–2007: U.S. Geological Survey Scientific Investigations Report 2009–5070, 86 p.; also available at *http://pubs.usgs.gov/sir/2009/5070/.*

Torak, L.J., and McDowell, R.J., 1996, Ground-water resources of the lower Apalachicola–Chattahoochee–Flint River Basin in parts of Alabama, Florida, and Georgia— Subarea 4 of the Apalachicola–Chattahoochee–Flint and Alabama–Coosa–Tallapoosa River Basins: U.S. Geological Survey Open-File Report 95–321, 145 p.

U.S. Environmental Protection Agency, 2000, Maximum contaminant levels (Subpart B of part 141, National Primary Drinking-Water Regulations): U.S. Code of Federal Regulations, Title 40, parts 100–149, revised as of July 1, 2000, p. 334–560.

U.S. Geological Survey, 2008, Georgia's ground-water resources and monitoring network, 2008: U.S. Geological Survey Fact Sheet 2008–3072, p. 2; Web-only publication available at *http://pubs.usgs.gov/fs/2008/3072/.*

Appendix A.   Groundwater-Level Hydrographs and Statistics for Continuously Monitored Recorder Wells and Wells Measured Periodically for 2008 and Period of Record in the Albany Area of Dougherty County, Georgia

Surficial Aquifer

31301908410402   Site Name: 12L371

Latitude: 31°30'19" Longitude: 84°10'46"   Dougherty County   Period of Record: 2003 - 2008
          Well Depth: 44.1 feet   Datum: 191 feet   Well Diameter: 2 inches

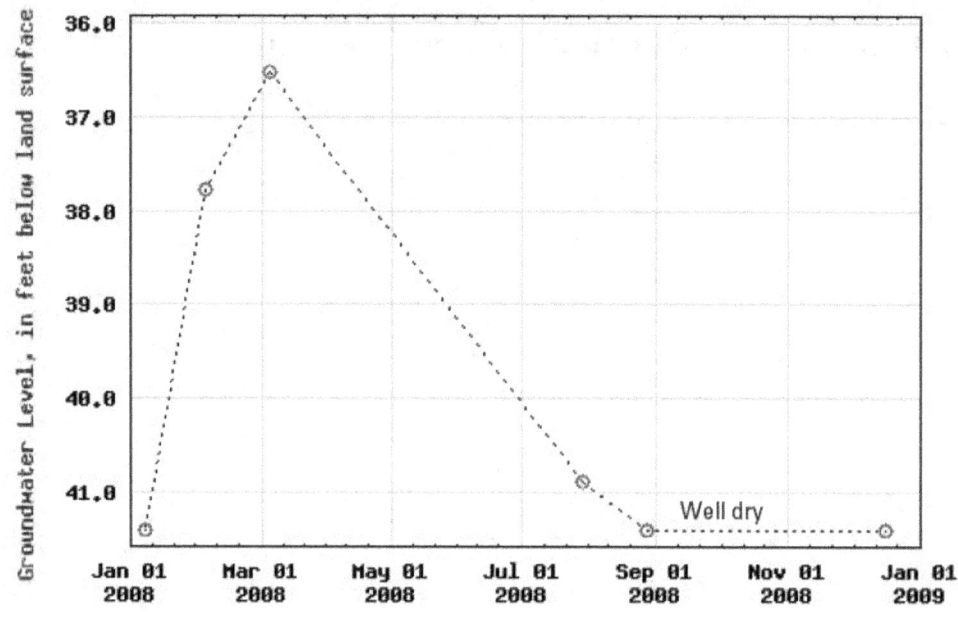

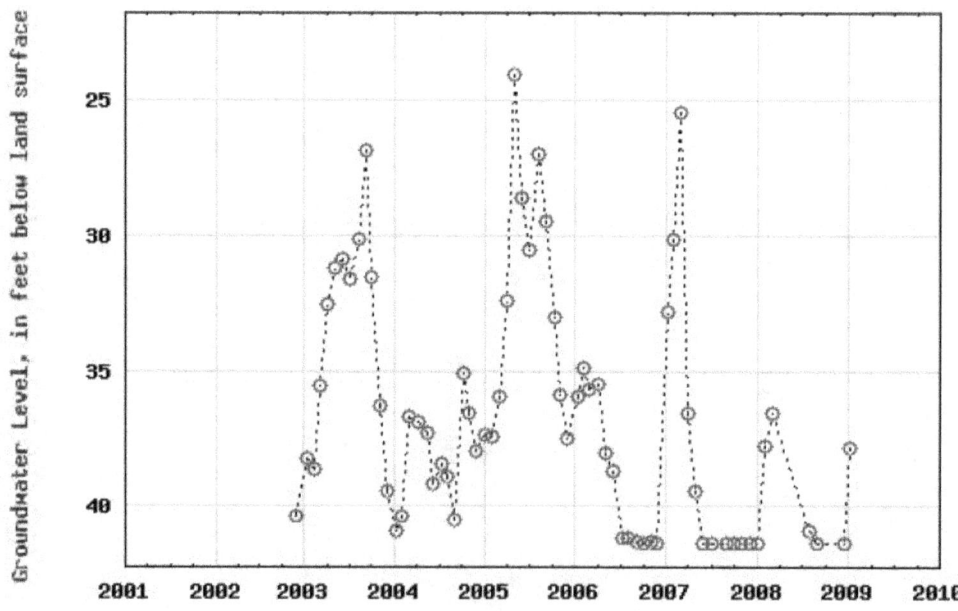

Figure A–1.   Periodic water levels in well 12L371, surficial aquifer, 2003–2008.

Surficial Aquifer

313038084122501   Site Name: 12L376

Latitude: 31° 30' 42" Longitude: 84°12'33"   Dougherty County   Period of Record: 2002 - 2008
         Well Depth: 45 feet   Datum: 191 feet   Well Diameter: 2 inches

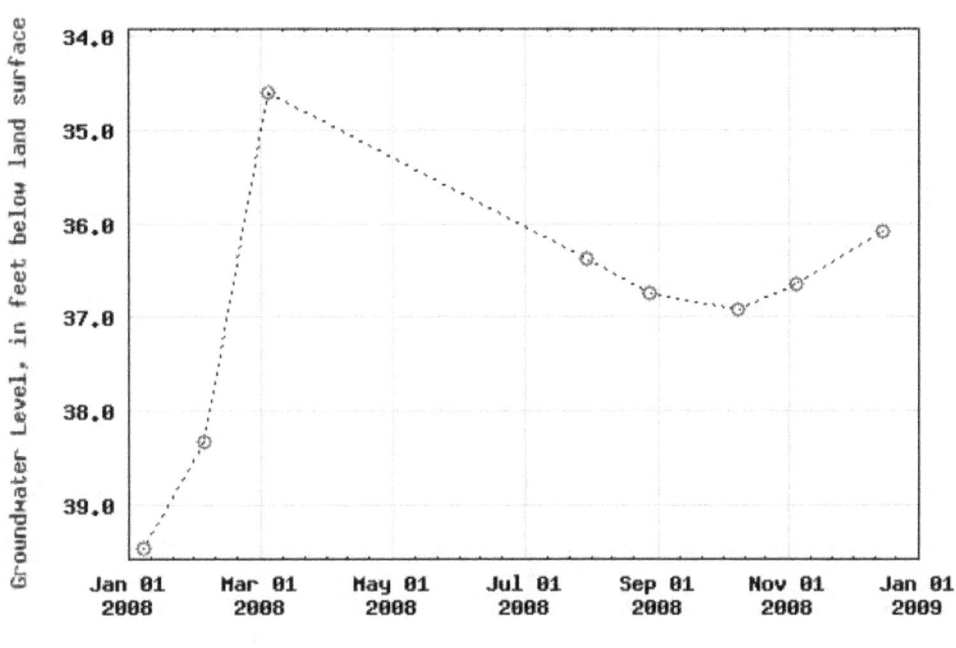

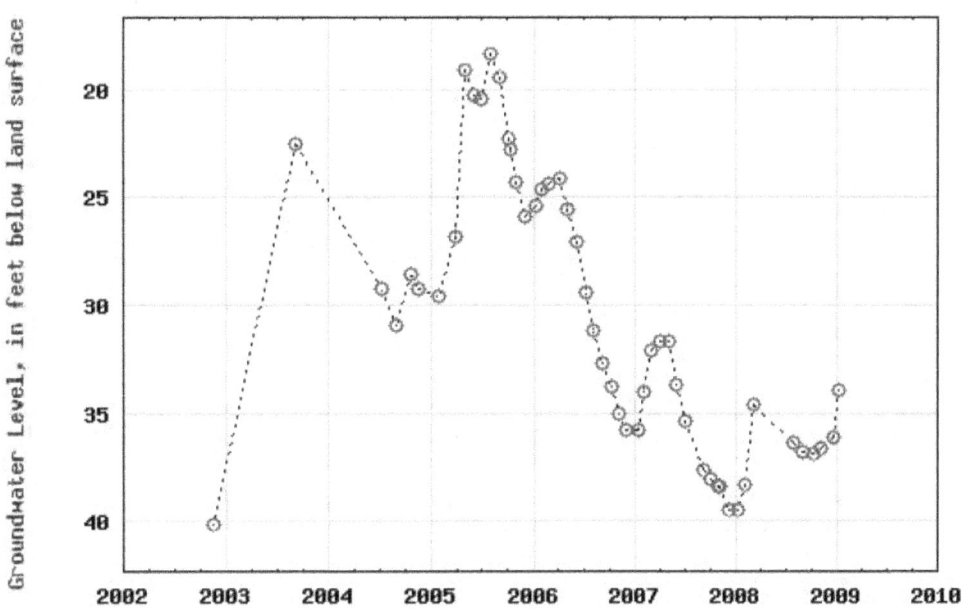

Figure A–2.   Periodic water levels in well 12L376, surficial aquifer, 2002–2008.

Upper Floridan Aquifer

312919084153801   Site Name: 11K003

Latitude: 31° 29' 15" Longitude: 84°15 31"   Dougherty County   Period of Record: 1979 - 2008
          Well Depth: 150 feet   Datum: 195 feet   Well Diameter: 4 inches

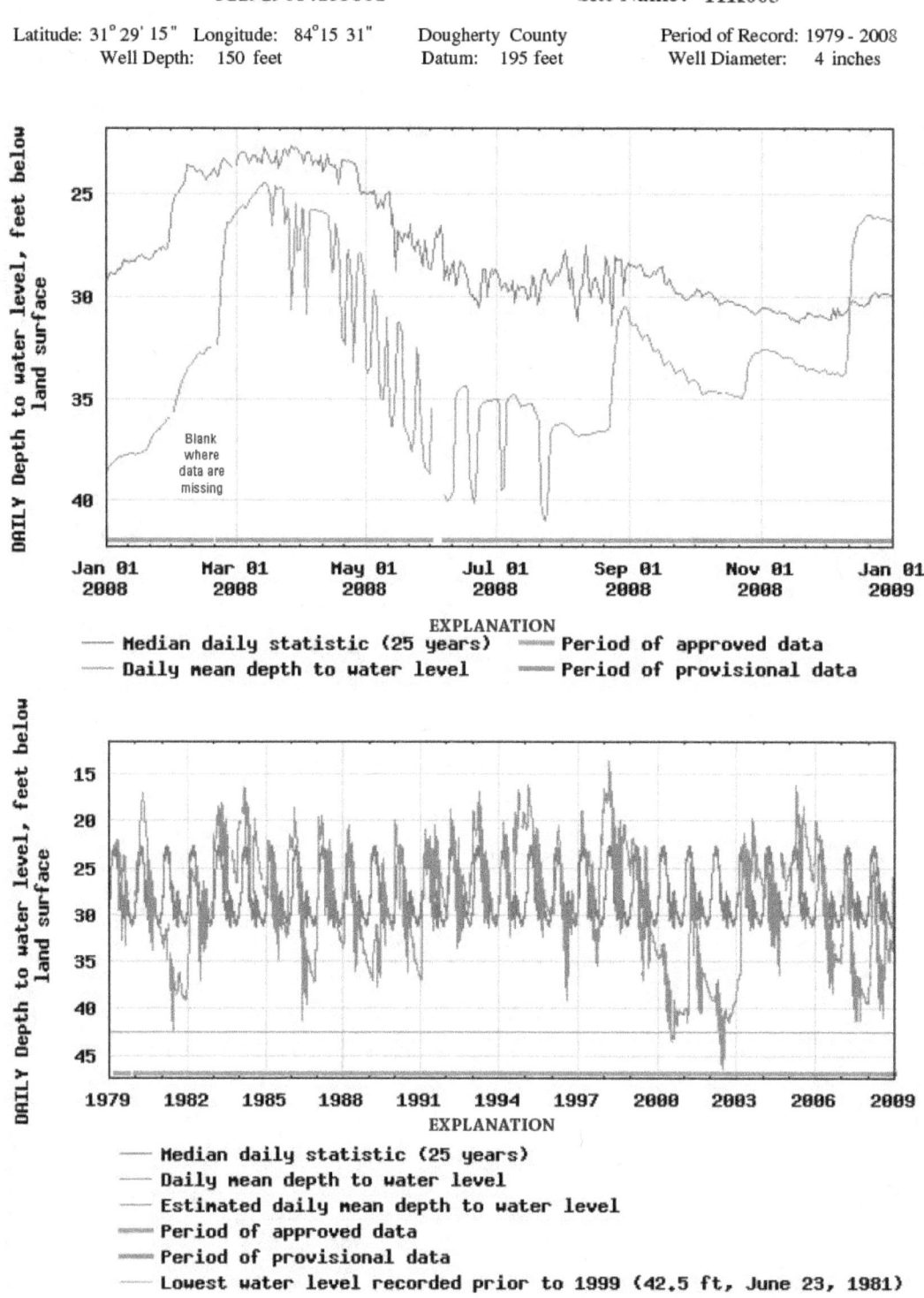

EXPLANATION
—— Median daily statistic (25 years)   ▥▥▥ Period of approved data
—— Daily mean depth to water level   ▬▬▬ Period of provisional data

EXPLANATION
—— Median daily statistic (25 years)
—— Daily mean depth to water level
—— Estimated daily mean depth to water level
▥▥ Period of approved data
▬▬ Period of provisional data
—— Lowest water level recorded prior to 1999 (42.5 ft, June 23, 1981)

Figure A–3.   Periodic and daily mean water levels in well 11K003, Upper Floridan aquifer, 1979–2008.

Upper Floridan Aquifer

312617084110701   **Site Name: 12K014**

Latitude: 31° 26' 12" Longitude: 84° 11 05"   Baker County   Period of Record: 1982 - 2008
          Well Depth: 137 feet   Datum: 185 feet   Well Diameter: 2 inches

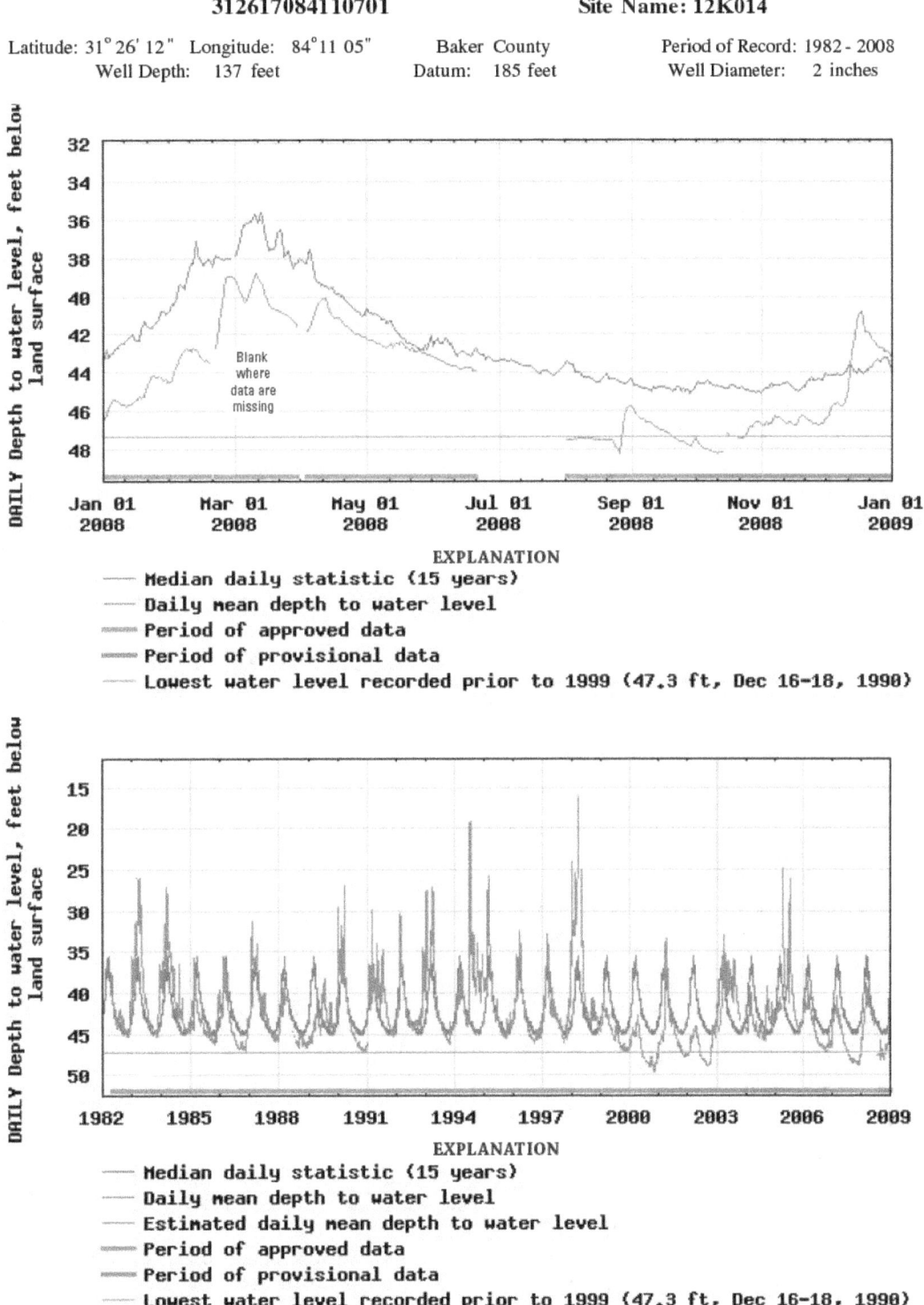

Figure A–4.   Periodic and daily mean water levels in well 12K014, Upper Floridan aquifer, 1982–2008.

Upper Floridan Aquifer

312950084131801   Site Name: 12K141

Latitude: 31° 29' 51" Longitude: 84°13 18"   Dougherty County   Period of Record: 1997 - 2008
            Well Depth: 200 feet   Datum: 195 feet   Well Diameter: 4 inches

EXPLANATION
—— Median daily statistic (9 years)   ═══ Period of approved data
—— Daily mean depth to water level   ═══ Period of provisional data

EXPLANATION
—— Median daily statistic (9 years)   ═══ Period of approved data
—— Daily mean depth to water level   ═══ Period of provisional data

Figure A–5. Periodic and daily mean water levels in well 12K141, Upper Floridan aquifer, 1997–2008.

Upper Floridan Aquifer

312947084092201   **Site Name: 12K180**

Latitude: 31° 29' 46" Longitude: 84°09 22"   Dougherty County   Period of Record: 2003-2008
        Well Depth: 170 feet   Datum: 172 feet   Well Diameter: 4 inches

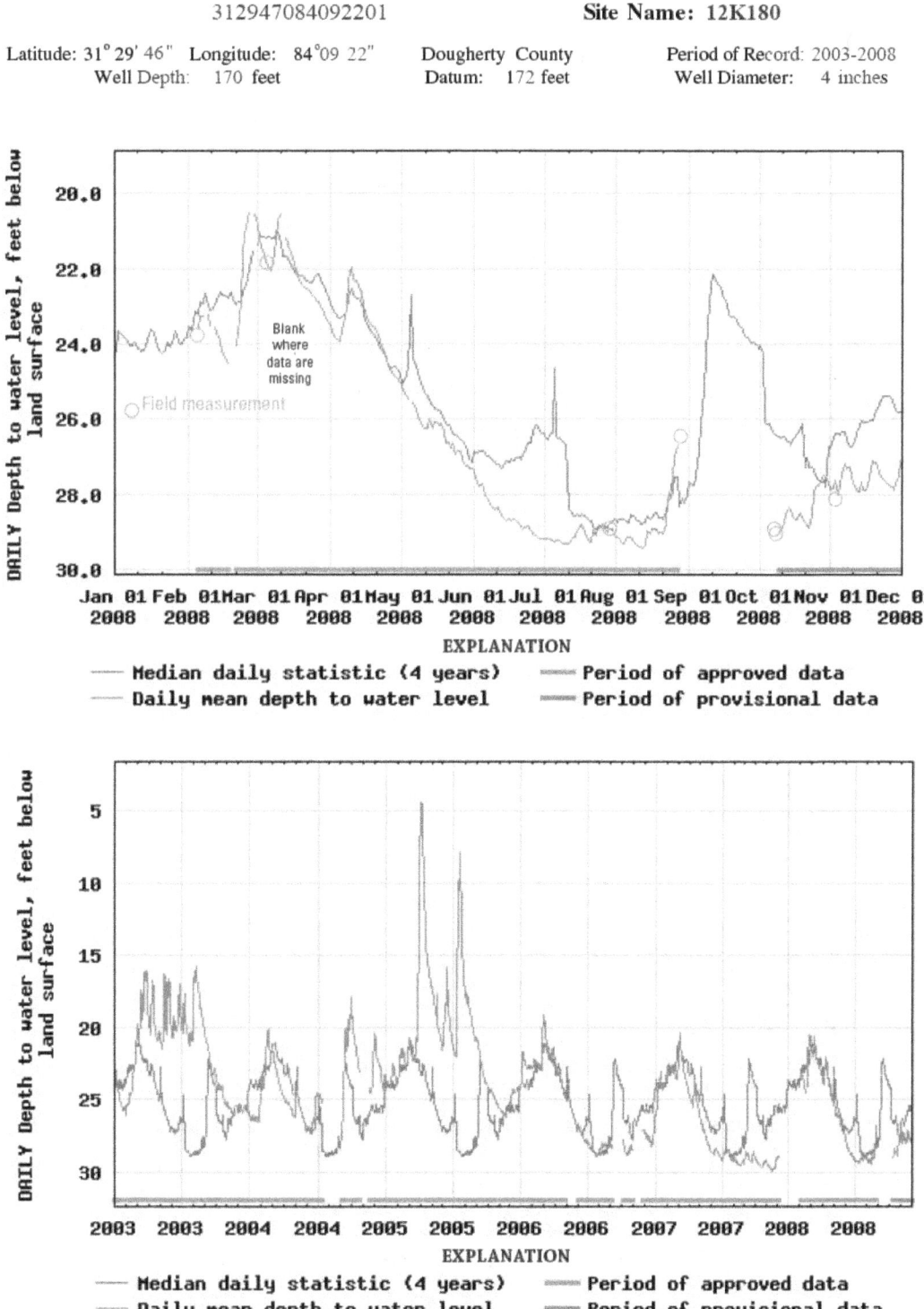

Figure A–6.   Periodic and daily mean water levels in well 12K180, Upper Floridan aquifer, 2003–2008.

Upper Floridan Aquifer

313450084091801   Site Name: **12L029**

Latitude: 31° 34' 51" Longitude: 84°09 18"   Dougherty County   Period of Record: 1983 - 2008
        Well Depth: 178 feet   Datum: 198 feet   Well Diameter: 6 inches

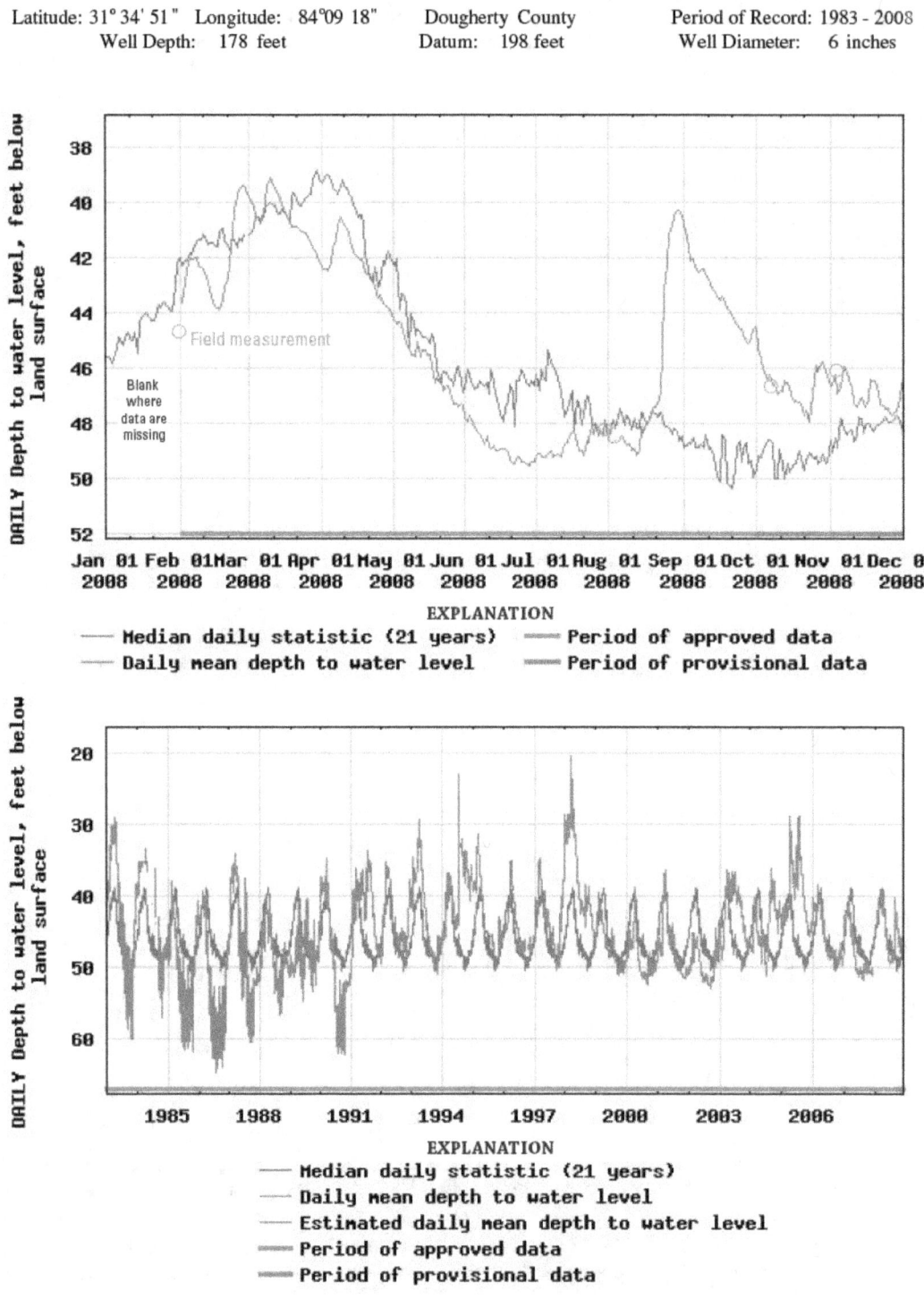

Figure A–7.   Periodic and daily mean water levels in well 12L029, Upper Floridan aquifer, 1983–2008.

Upper Floridan Aquifer

313130084101001   **Site Name: 12L030**

Latitude: 31° 31' 31"   Longitude: 84°10'10"   Dougherty County   Period of Record: 1985 - 2008
        Well Depth: 180 feet   Datum: 179 feet   Well Diameter: 4 inches

Figure A–8.   Periodic and daily mean water levels in well 12L030, Upper Floridan aquifer, 1985–2008.

Upper Floridan Aquifer

313040084125901   Site Name: 12L277

Latitude: 31° 30' 41"   Longitude: 84°12´59"   Dougherty County   Period of Record: 1998 - 2008
Well Depth: 203 feet   Datum: 185 feet   Well Diameter: 4 inches

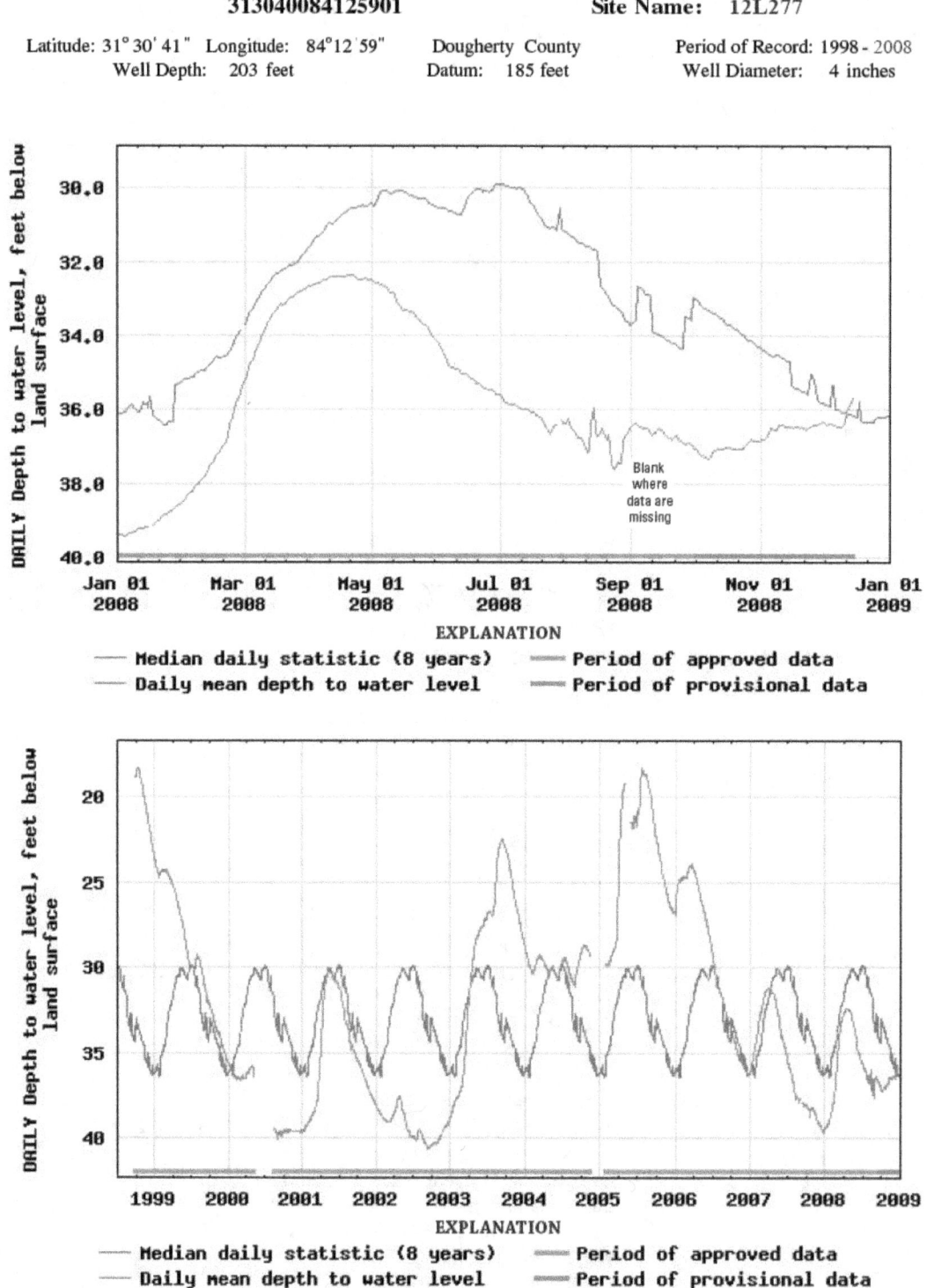

Figure A–9.   Periodic and daily mean water levels in well 12L277, Upper Floridan aquifer, 1998–2008.

Upper Floridan Aquifer

313019084104601   **Site Name: 12L370**

Latitude: 31° 30' 20" Longitude: 84°10'46"   Dougherty County   Period of Record: 2000 - 2008
              Well Depth: 172 feet   Datum: 190 feet   Well Diameter: 6 inches

EXPLANATION
── Median daily statistic (7 years)   ▒▒▒ Period of approved data
── Daily mean depth to water level   ▒▒▒ Period of provisional data

EXPLANATION
── Median daily statistic (7 years)   ▒▒▒ Period of approved data
── Daily mean depth to water level   ▒▒▒ Period of provisional data

Figure A–10.   Periodic and daily mean water levels in well 12L370, Upper Floridan aquifer, 2000–2008.

Upper Floridan Aquifer

313019084104603   Site Name: 12L372

Latitude: 31°30' 19" Longitude: 84°10 46"   Dougherty County   Period of Record: 2000 - 2008
              Well Depth: 58 feet   Datum: 188 feet   Well Diameter: 2 inches

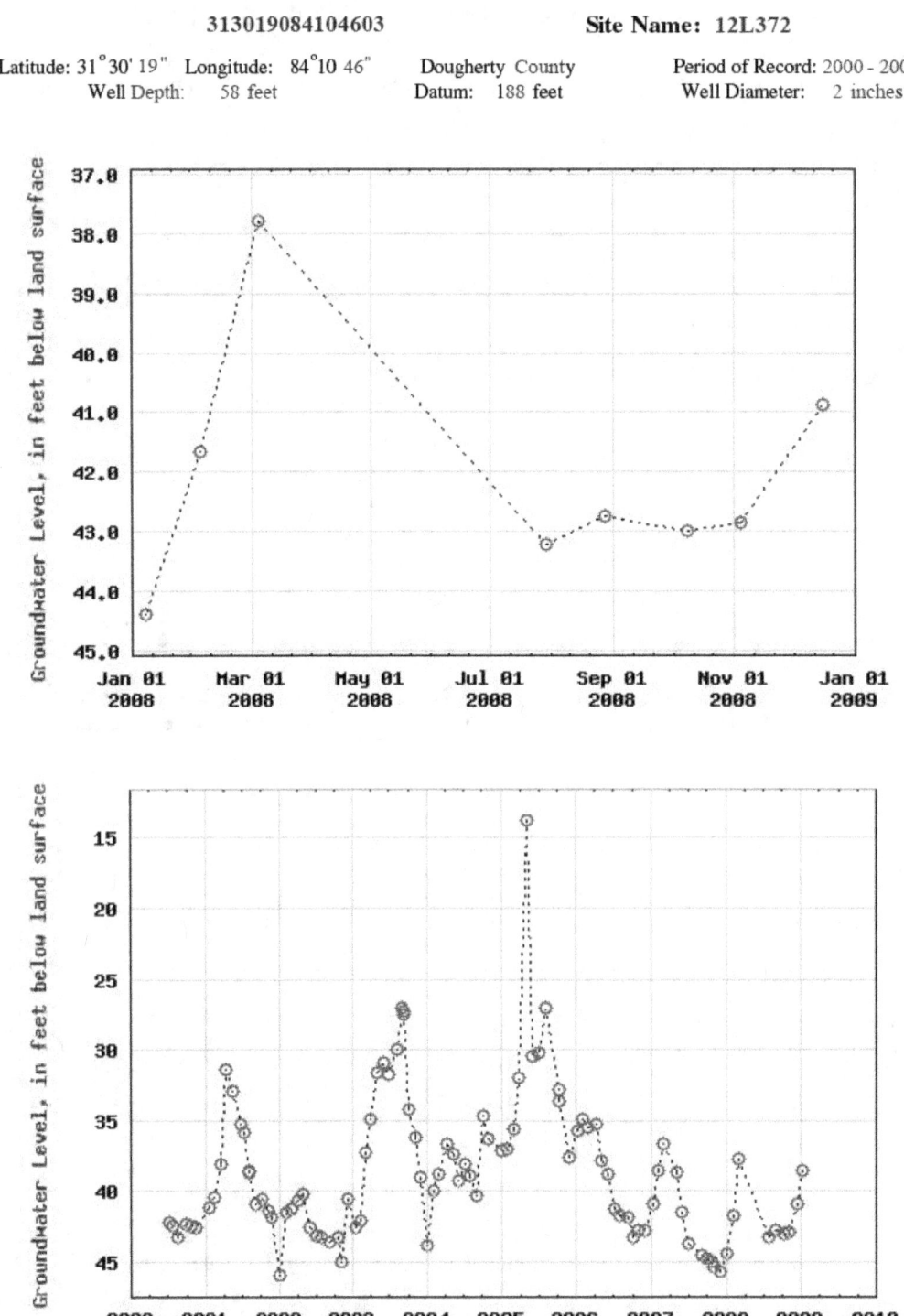

Figure A–11.   Periodic and daily mean water levels in well 12L372, Upper Floridan aquifer, 2000–2008.

Upper Floridan Aquifer

313000084100301   Site Name: 12L373

Latitude: 31° 30' 00" Longitude: 84°10 02"   Dougherty County   Period of Record: 2003 - 2008
            Well Depth: 170 feet   Datum: 186 feet   Well Diameter: 4 inches

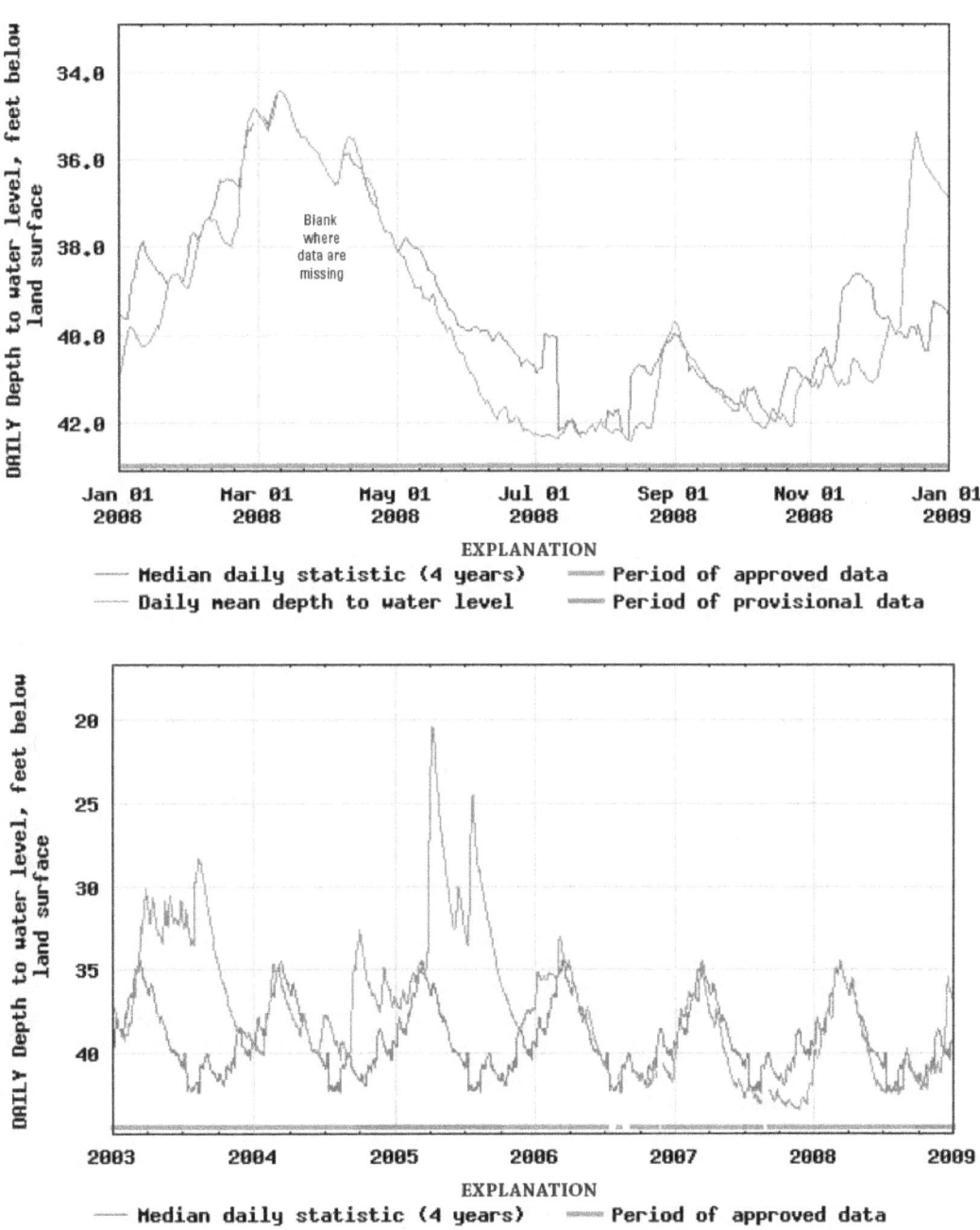

Figure A–12.   Periodic and daily mean water levels in well 12L373, Upper Floridan aquifer, 2003–2008.

Upper Floridan Aquifer

313808084093601   Site Name: 12M017

Latitude: 31° 38 ' 09" Longitude: 84°09 ' 36"   Lee County   Period of Record: 1982 - 2008
         Well Depth: 181 feet   Datum: 225 feet   Well Diameter: 4 inches

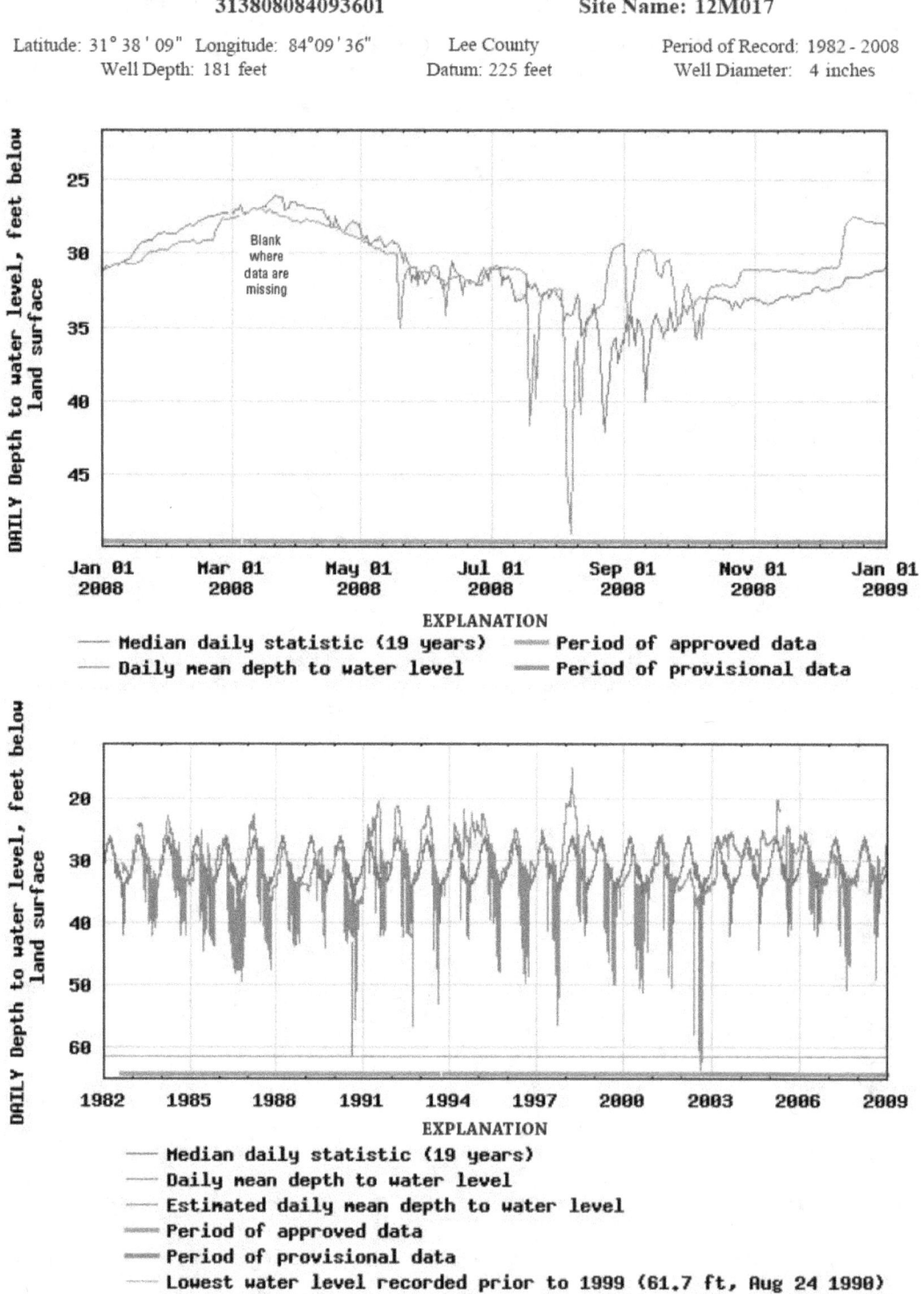

Figure A–13.   Periodic and daily mean water levels in well 12M017, Upper Floridan aquifer, 1982–2008.

Upper Floridan Aquifer

312704084071601   Site Name: 13K014

Latitude: 31° 27' 05" Longitude: 84°07'16"   Dougherty County   Period of Record: 1982 - 2008
          Well Depth: 131 feet   Datum: 180 feet   Well Diameter: 4 inches

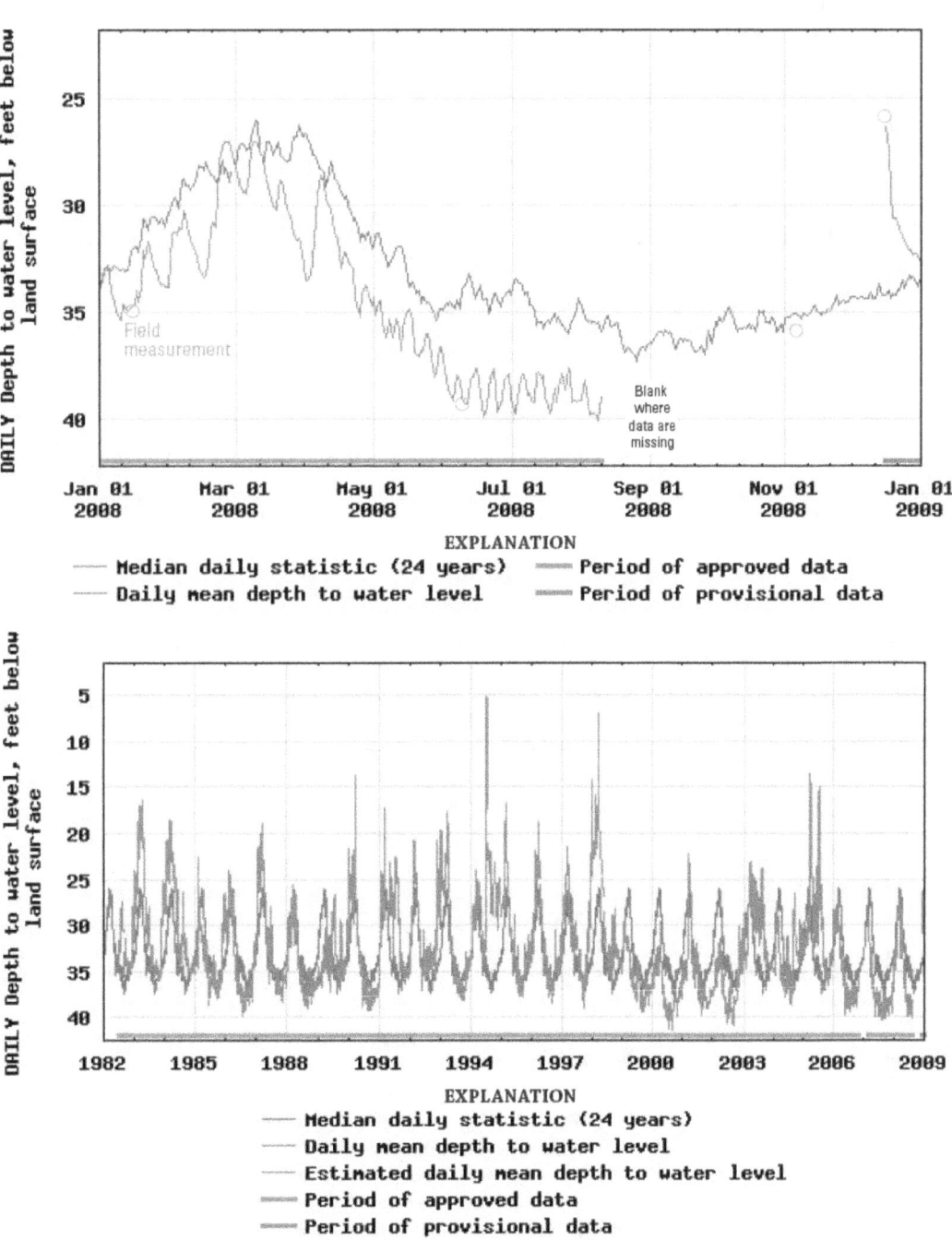

Figure A–14.   Periodic and daily mean water levels in well 13K014, Upper Floridan aquifer, 1982–2008.

Upper Floridan Aquifer

313105084064302   Site Name: 13L012

Latitude: 31° 31 ' 06" Longitude: 84°06 ' 43"   Dougherty County   Period of Record: 1977 - 2008
Well Depth: 218 feet   Datum: 195 feet   Well Diameter: 4 inches

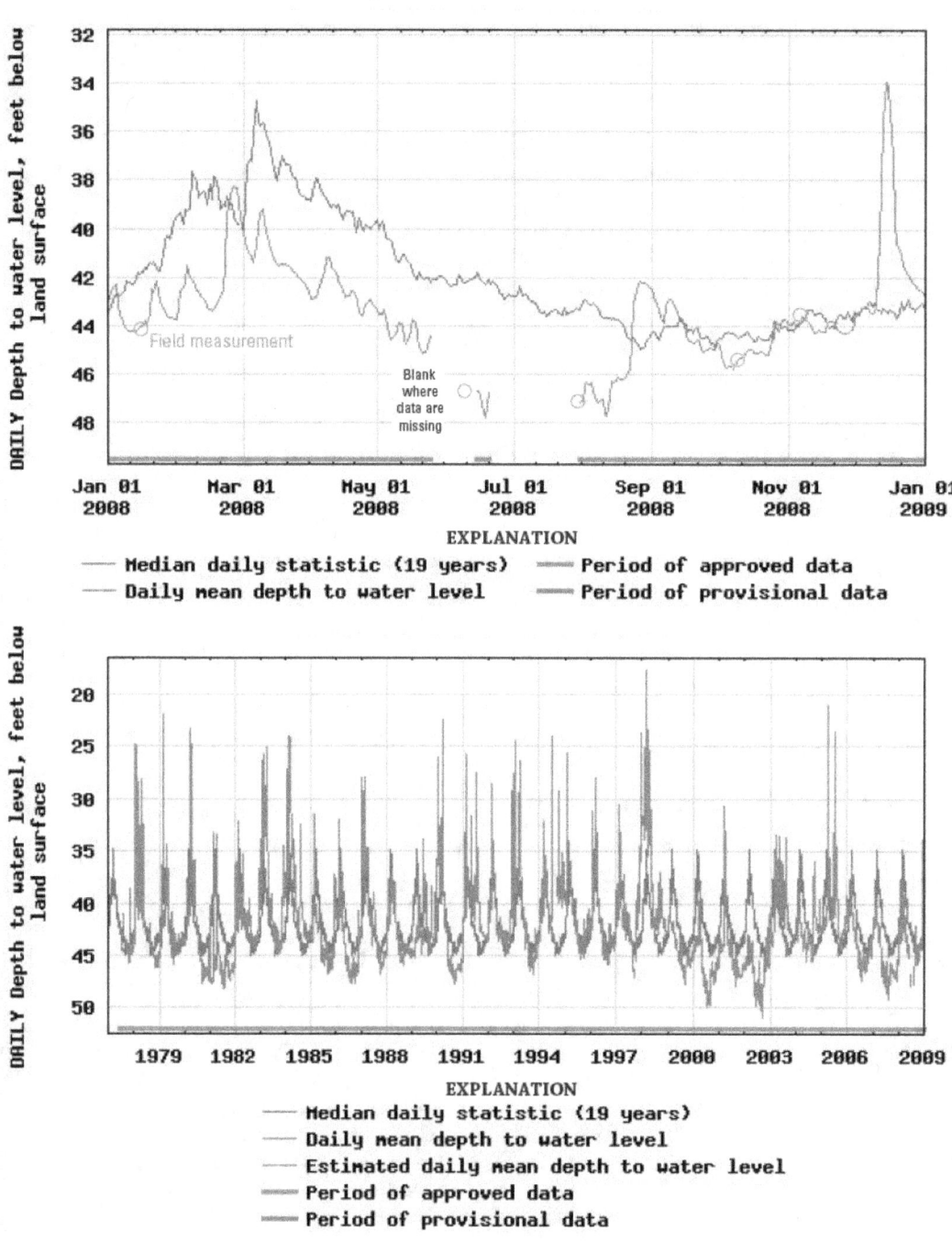

Figure A–15.   Periodic and daily mean water levels in well 13L012, Upper Floridan aquifer, 1977–2008.

Upper Floridan Aquifer

313521084051001   Site Name: 13L049

Latitude: 31° 35 ′ 22″ Longitude: 84°05′10″   Dougherty County   Period of Record: 1985 - 2008
Well Depth: 170 feet   Datum: 205 feet   Well Diameter: 6 inches

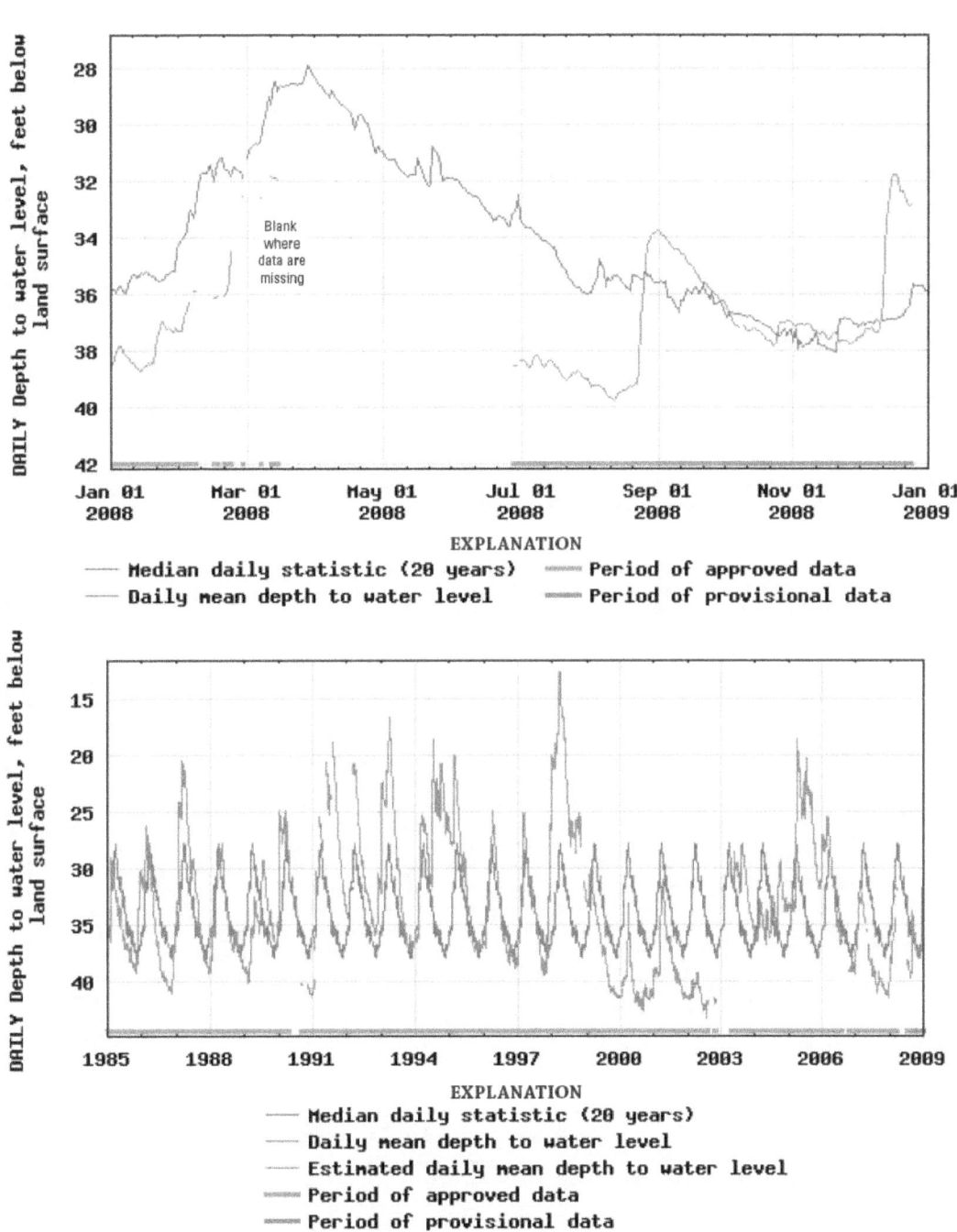

Figure A–16.   Periodic and daily mean water levels in well 13L049, Upper Floridan aquifer, 1985–2008.

Upper Floridan Aquifer

313247084005001   Site Name: 13L180

Latitude: 31° 32 ' 48" Longitude: 84°00' 50"   Dougherty County   Period of Record: 1996 - 2008
Well Depth: 310 feet   Datum: 230 feet   Well Diameter: 4 inches

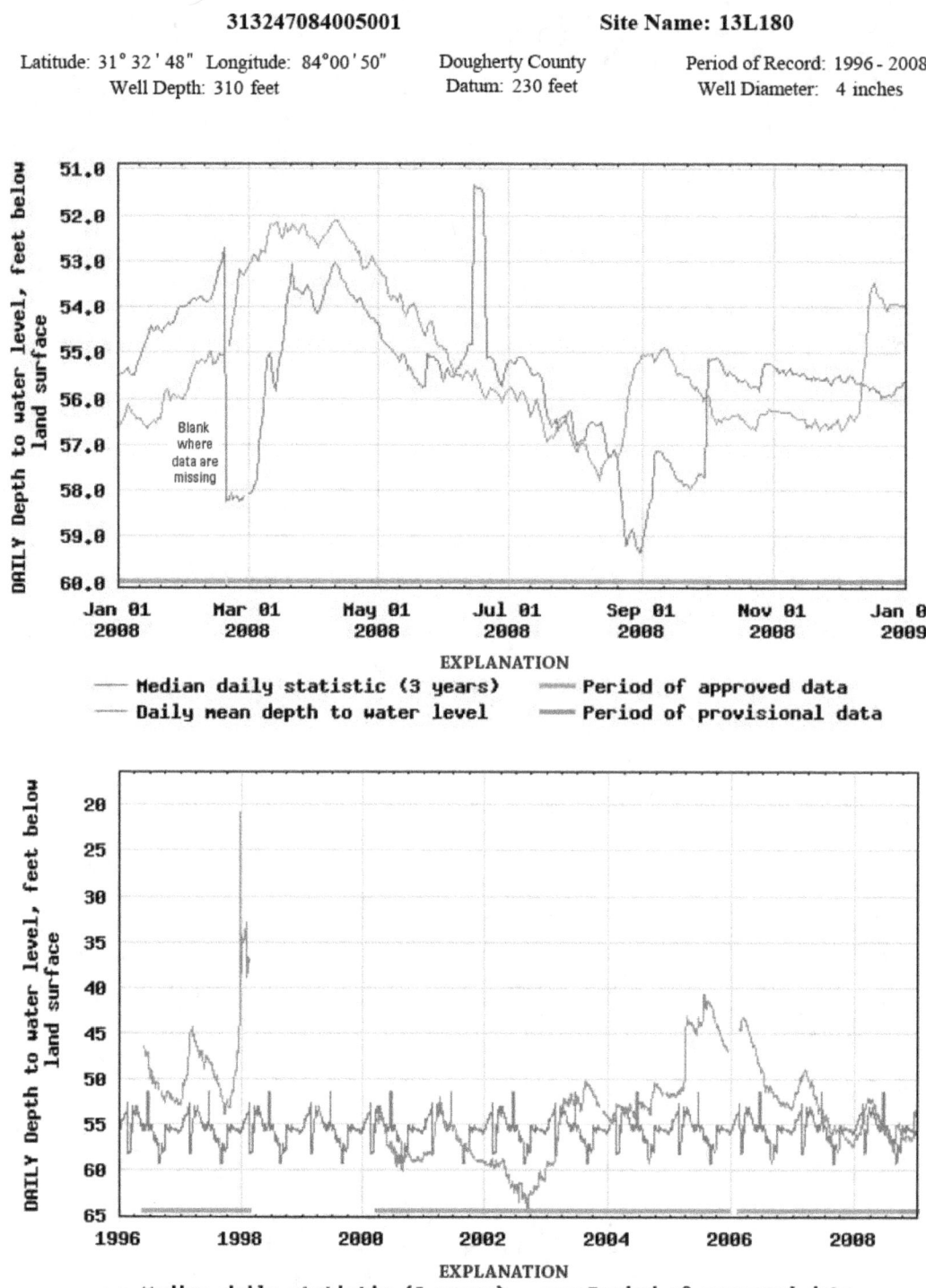

Figure A–17.   Periodic and daily mean water levels in well 13L180, Upper Floridan aquifer, 1996–2008.

Claiborne Aquifer

313534084103001   Site Name: 12L019

Latitude: 31° 35 ' 37" Longitude: 84° 10 ' 30"   Dougherty County   Period of Record: 1978 - 2008
Well Depth: 257 feet   Datum: 195 feet   Well Diameter: 6 inches

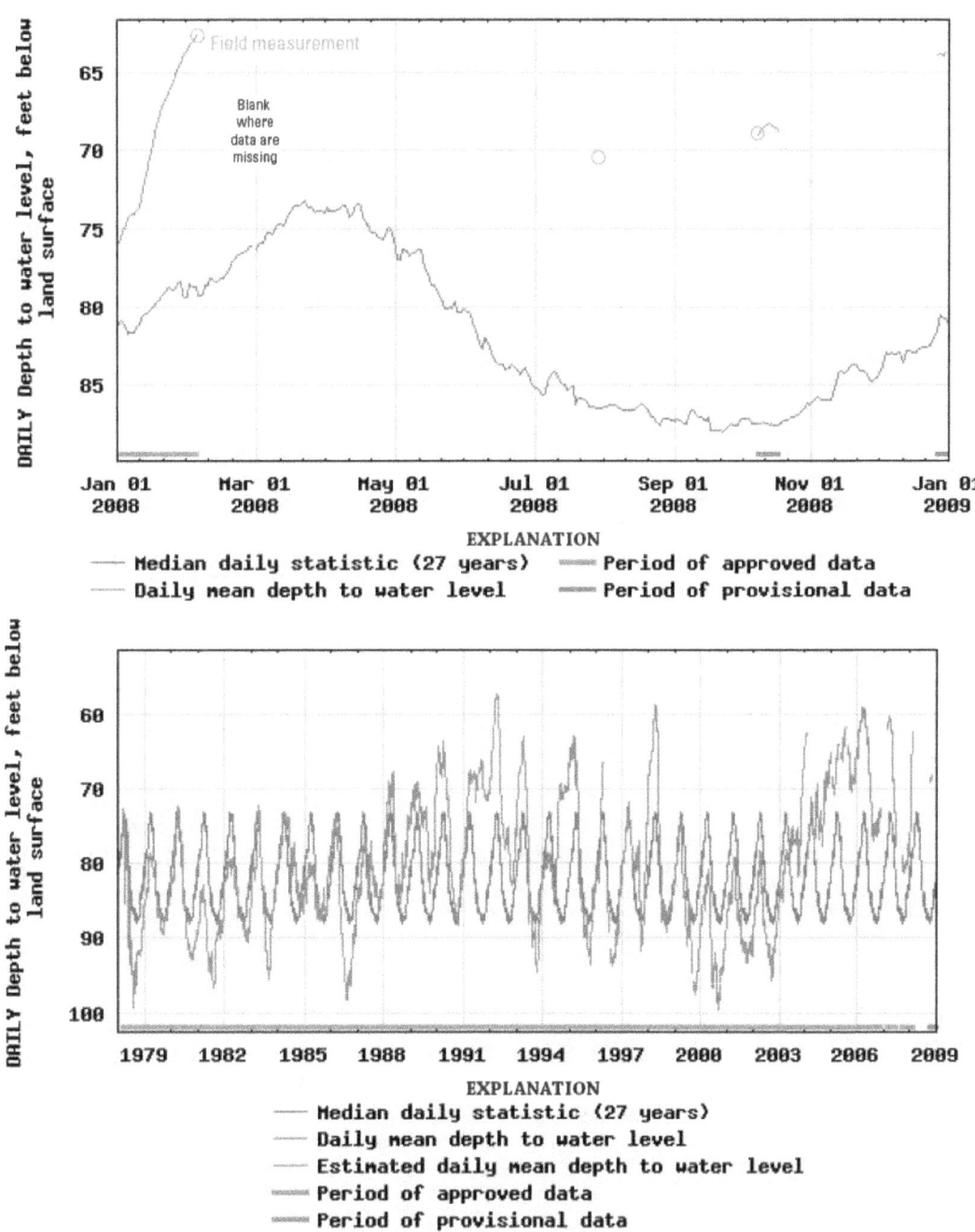

Figure A–18.   Periodic and daily mean water levels in well 12L019, Claiborne aquifer, 1978–2008.

Claiborne Aquifer

313105084064301   Site Name: 13L011

Latitude: 31° 31 ' 06" Longitude: 84°06'43"   Dougherty County   Period of Record: 1977 - 2008
            Well Depth: 418 feet   Datum: 195 feet   Well Diameter: 4 inches

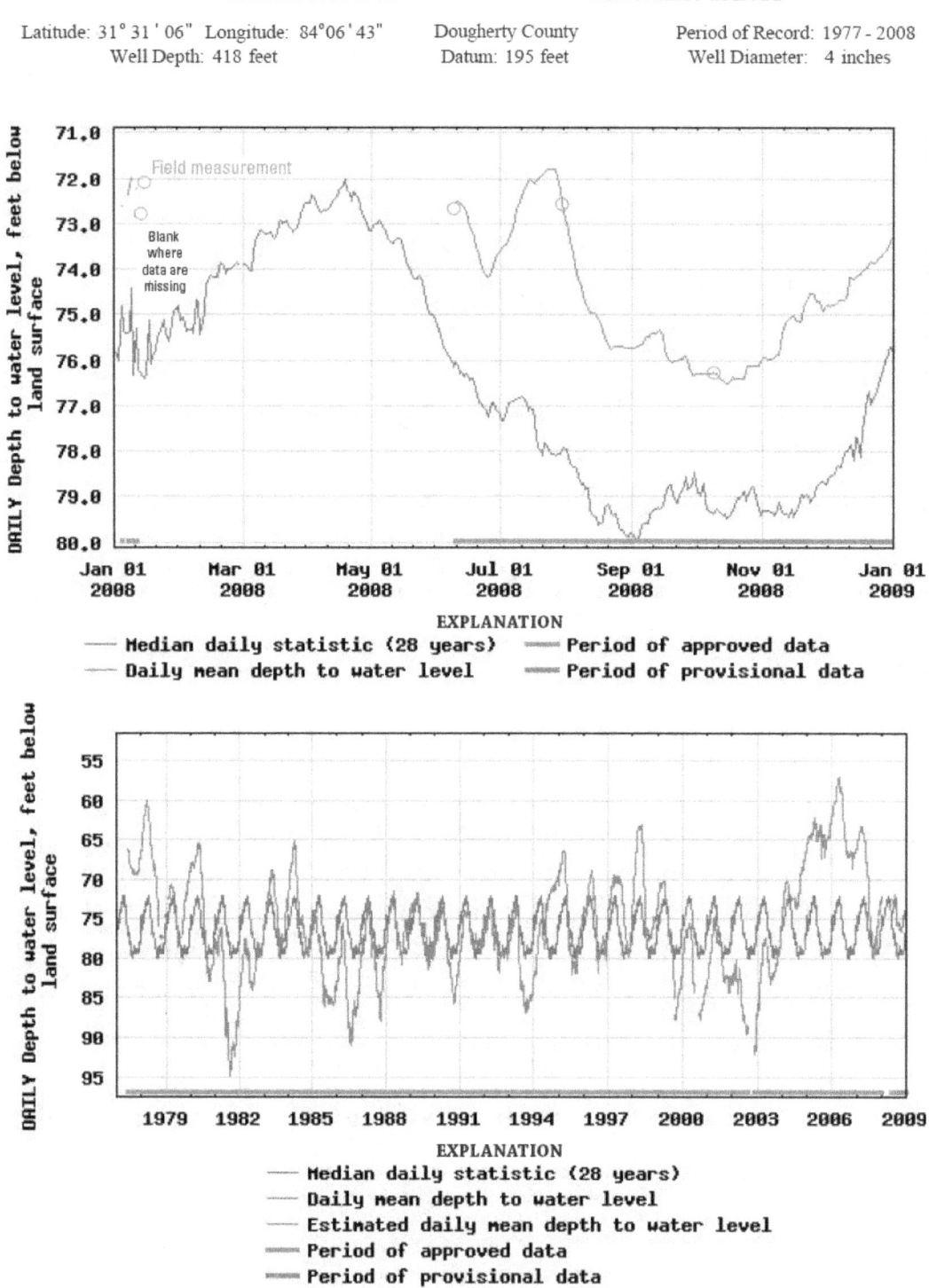

Figure A–19.   Periodic and daily mean water levels in well 13L011, Claiborne aquifer, 1977–2008.

Claiborne Aquifer

313625084041501   **Site Name: 13L015**

Latitude: 31° 36 ' 22" Longitude: 84°04 ' 09"   Dougherty County   Period of Record: 1979 - 2008
                     Well Depth: 351 feet   Datum: 200 feet   Well Diameter: 4 inches

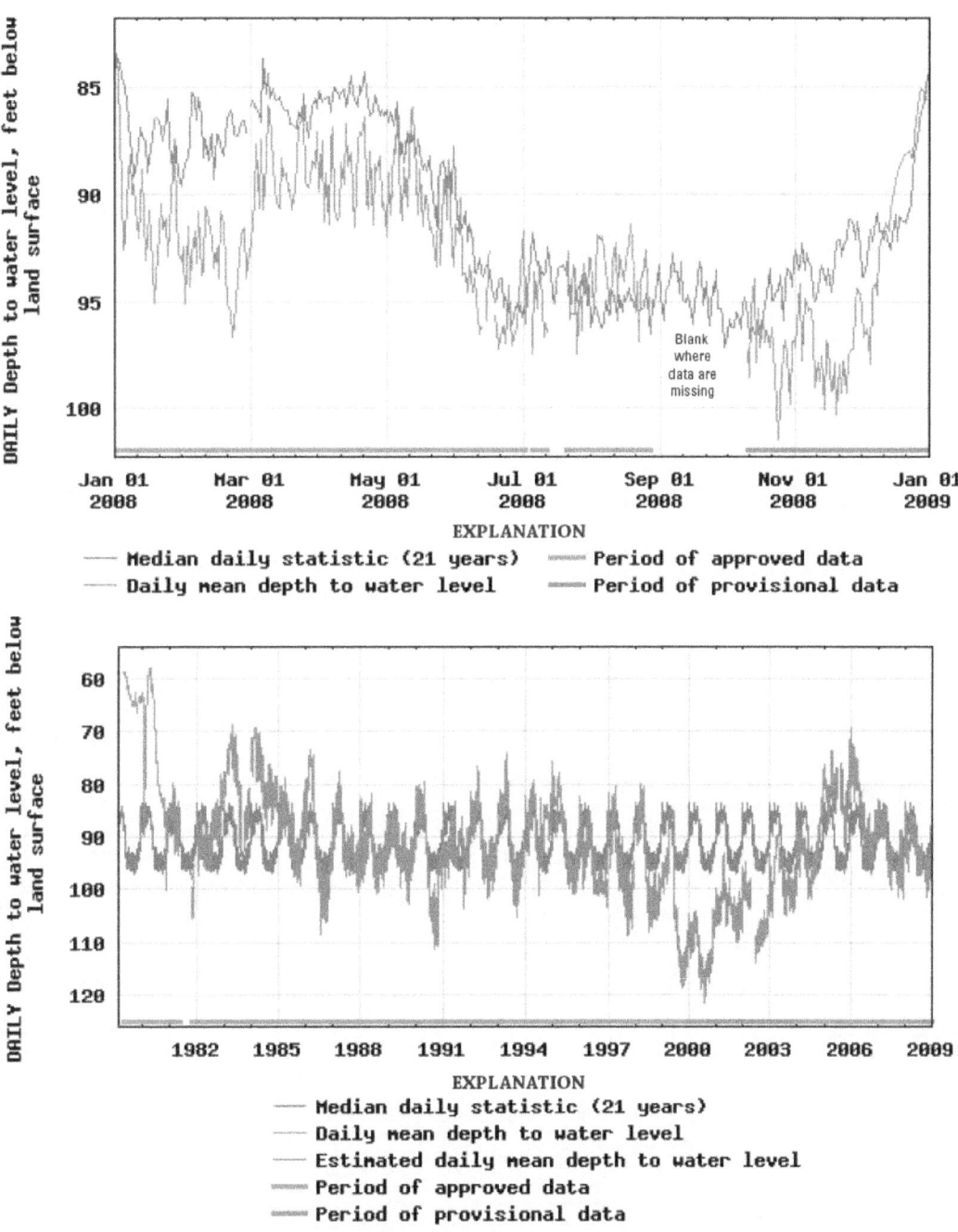

Figure A–20.   Periodic and daily mean water levels in well 13L015, Claiborne aquifer, 1979–2008.

Claiborne Aquifer

312654084210102   Site Name: 11K002

Latitude: 31° 26' 54" Longitude: 84°21'01"   Dougherty County   Period of Record: 1979 - 2008
         Well Depth: 320 feet   Datum: 183 feet   Well Diameter: 6 inches

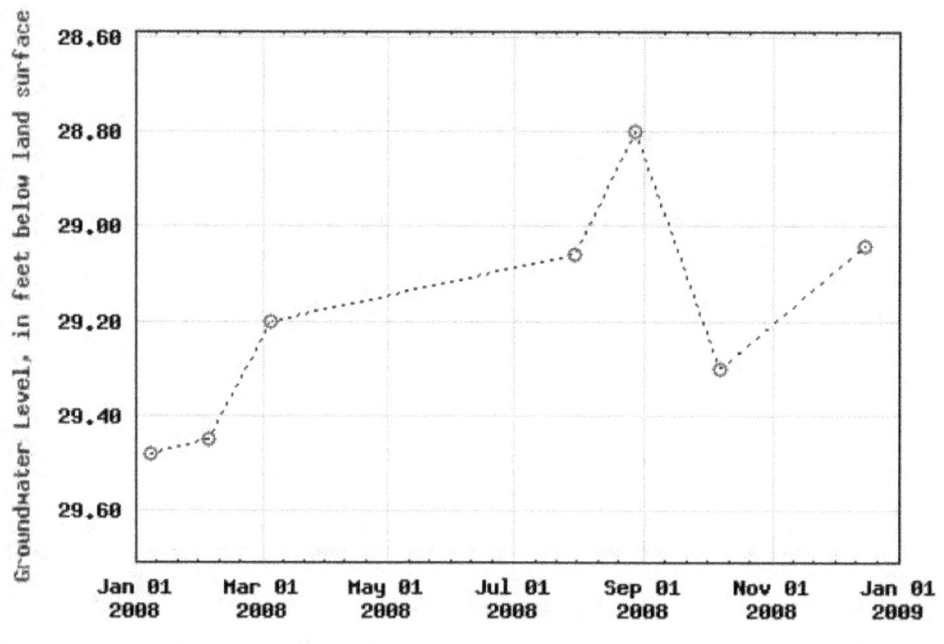

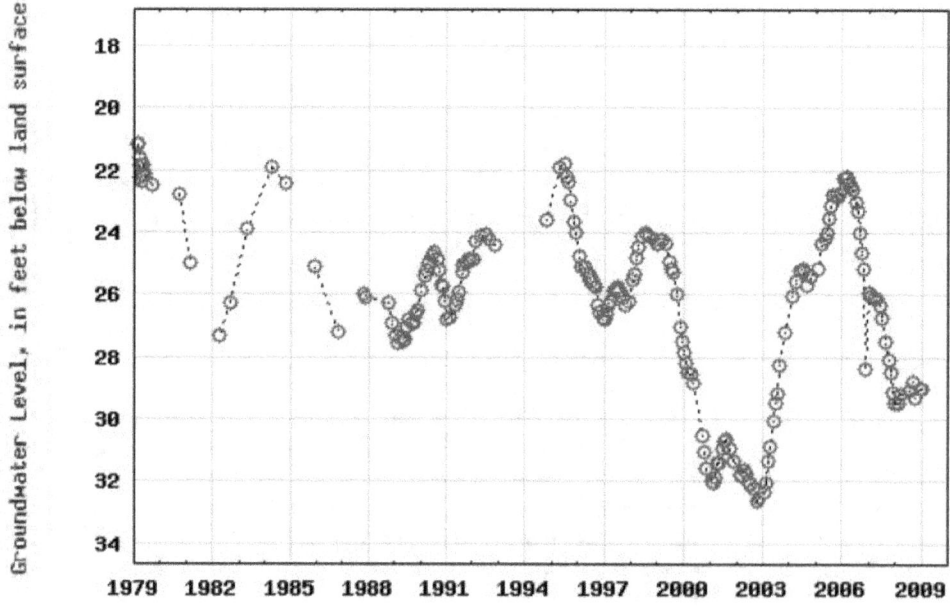

Figure A–21.   Periodic water levels in well 11K002, Claiborne aquifer, 1979–2008.

Claiborne Aquifer

313530084203202   **Site Name: 11L001**

Latitude: 31°35' 30" Longitude: 84°20' 34"   Dougherty County   Period of Record: 1978 - 2008
            Well Depth: 251 feet   Datum: 220 feet   Well Diameter: 4 inches

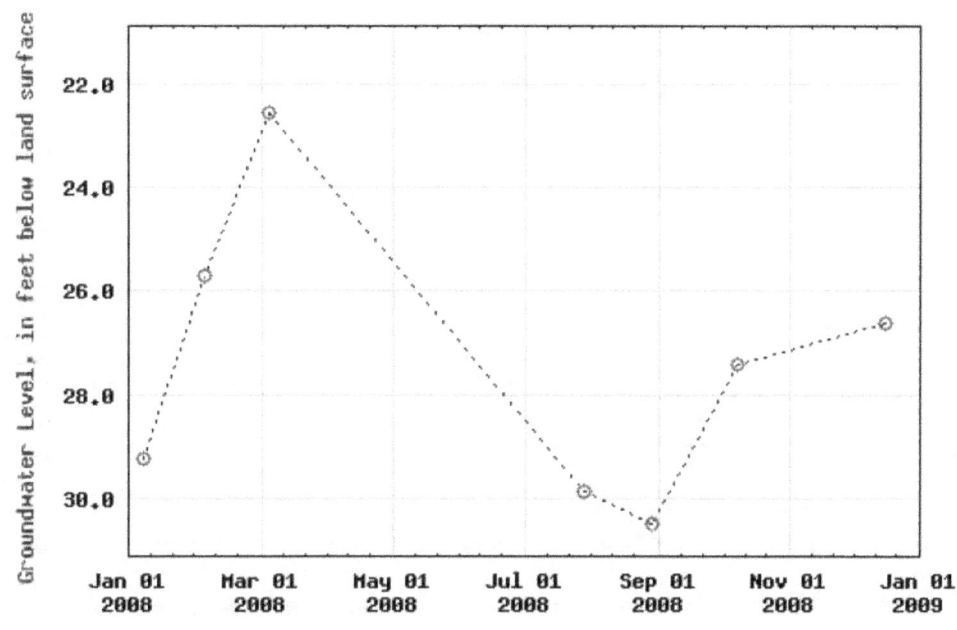

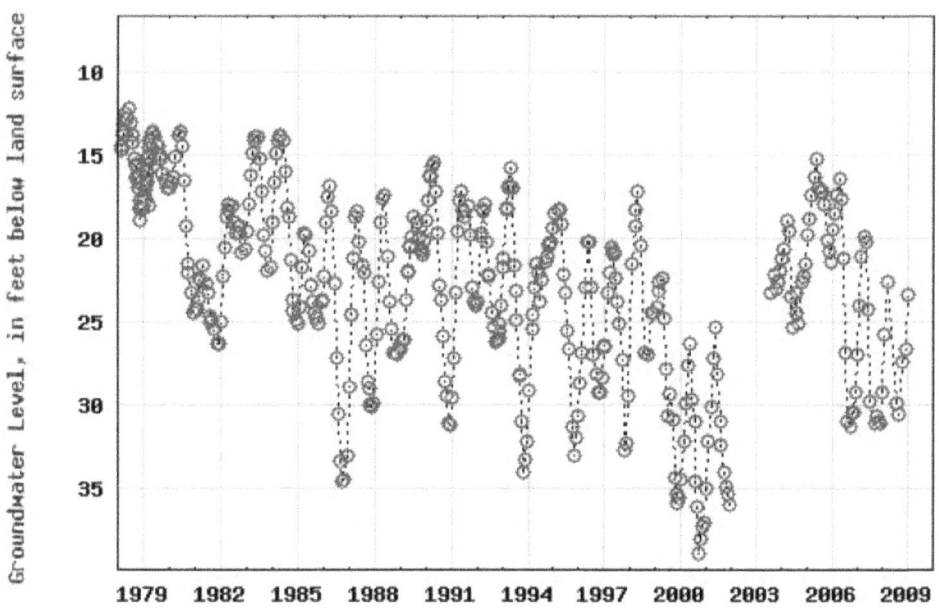

Figure A–22.   Periodic water levels in well 11L001, Claiborne aquifer, 1978–2008.

Clayton Aquifer

312654084210103   Site Name: 11K005

Latitude: 31° 26' 55" Longitude: 84°21'01"   Dougherty County   Period of Record: 1979 - 2008
Well Depth: 646 feet   Datum: 180 feet   Well Diameter: 6 inches

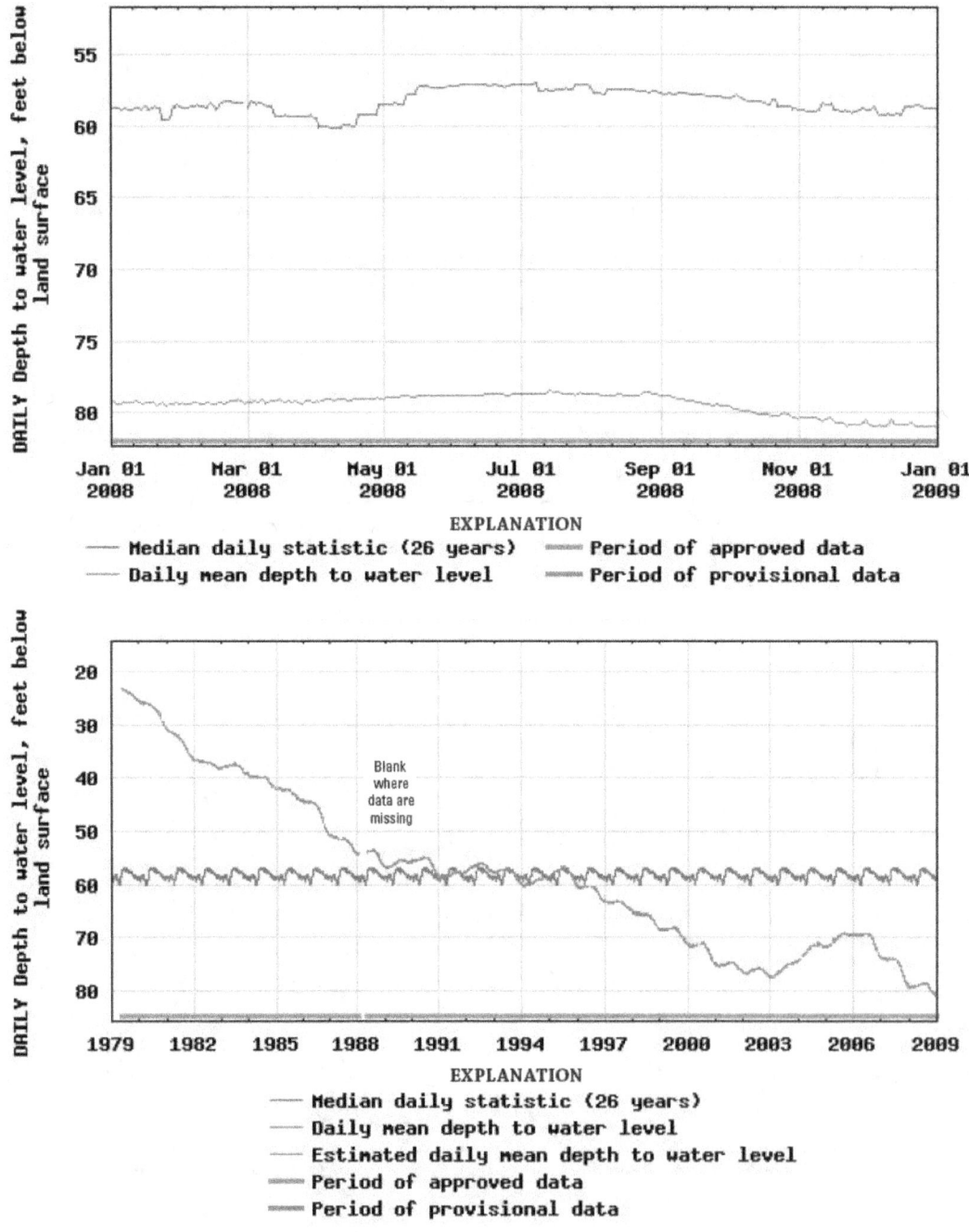

Figure A–23.   Periodic and daily mean water levels in well 11K005, Clayton aquifer, 1979–2008.

Clayton Aquifer

313532084203501   Site Name: 11L002

Latitude: 31°35'33" Longitude: 84°20'32"   Dougherty County   Period of Record: 1973 - 2008
Well Depth: 656 feet   Datum: 222 feet   Well Diameter: 3 inches

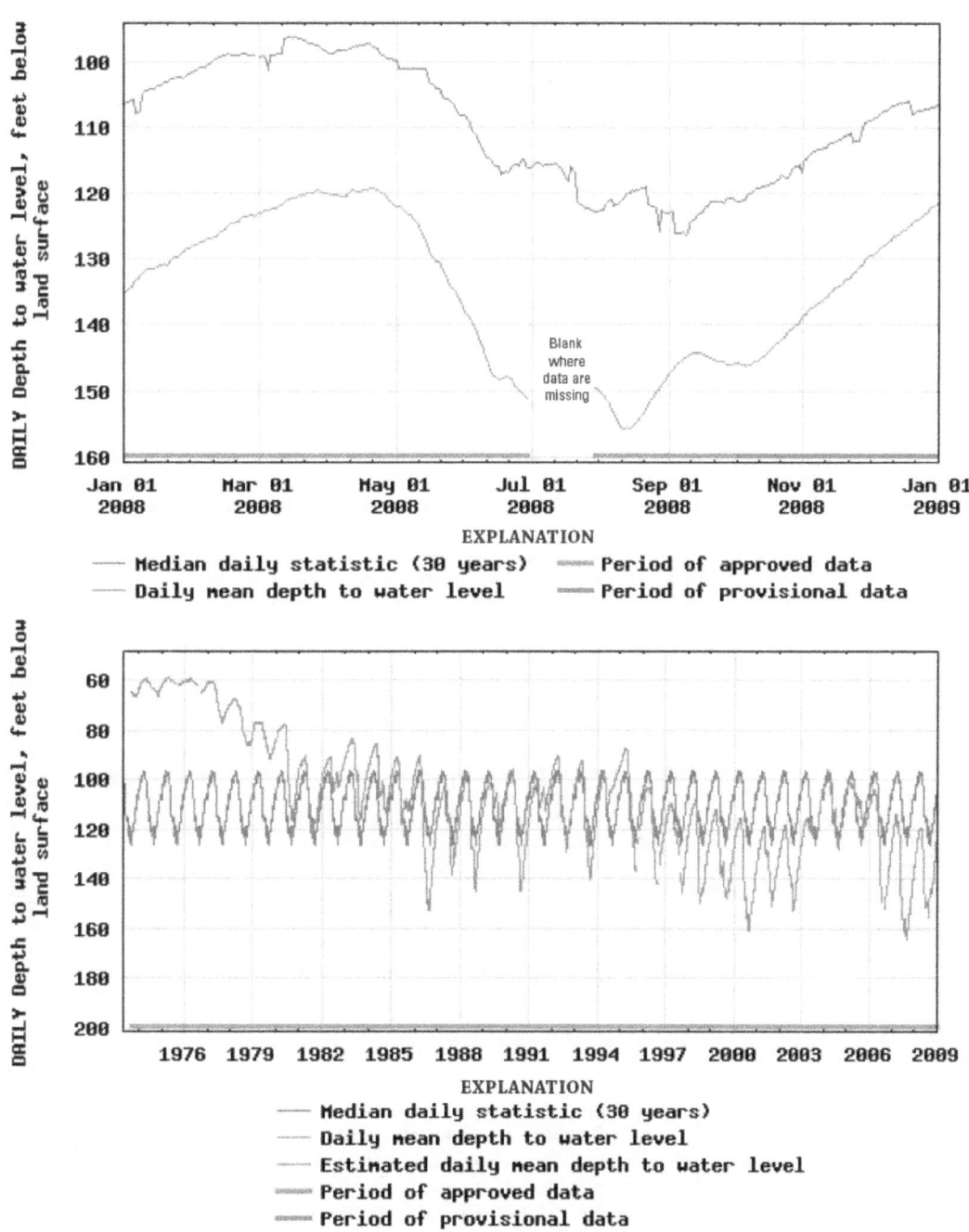

Figure A–24. Periodic and daily mean water levels in well 11L002, Clayton aquifer, 1973–2008.

Clayton Aquifer

313534084103002   Site Name: 12L020

Latitude: 31° 35′ 35″ Longitude: 24°10′30″   Lee County   Period of Record: 1978 - 2008
          Well Depth: 690 feet   Datum: 195 feet   Well Diameter: 4 inches

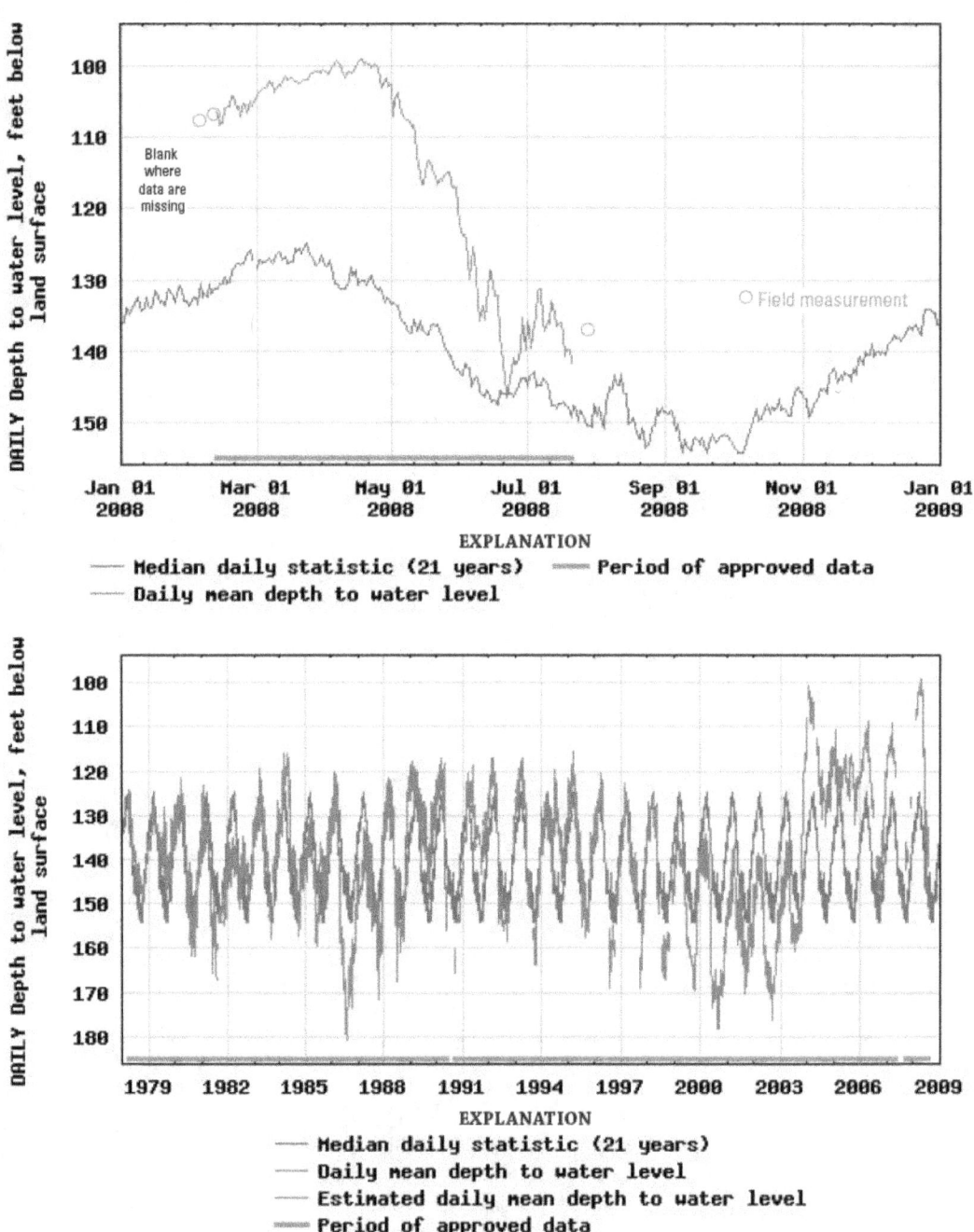

Figure A–25.   Periodic and daily mean water levels in well 12L020, Clayton aquifer, 1978–2008.

Clayton Aquifer

313812084125001   Site Name: 12M002

Latitude: 31°38'11" Longitude: 84°12'49"   Lee County   Period of Record: 1978 - 2008
          Well Depth: 650 feet   Datum: 240 feet   Well Diameter: 6 inches

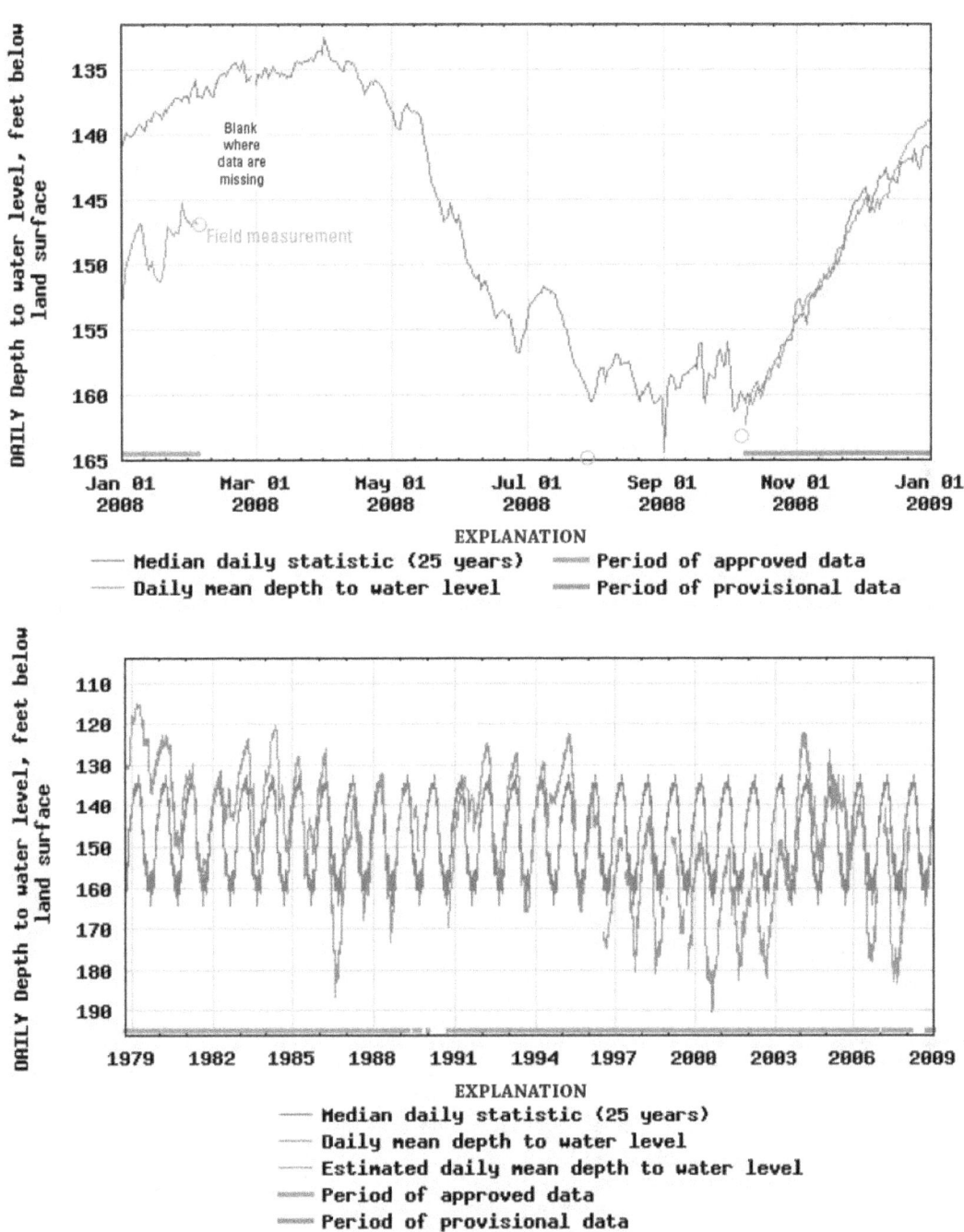

Figure A–26.   Periodic and daily mean water levels in well 12M002, Clayton aquifer, 1978–2008.

Clayton Aquifer

313554084062501   Site Name: 13L002

Latitude: 31°35'52" Longitude: 84°06'24"   Dougherty County   Period of Record: 1957 - 2008
Well Depth: 760 feet   Datum: 212 feet   Well Diameter: 12 inches

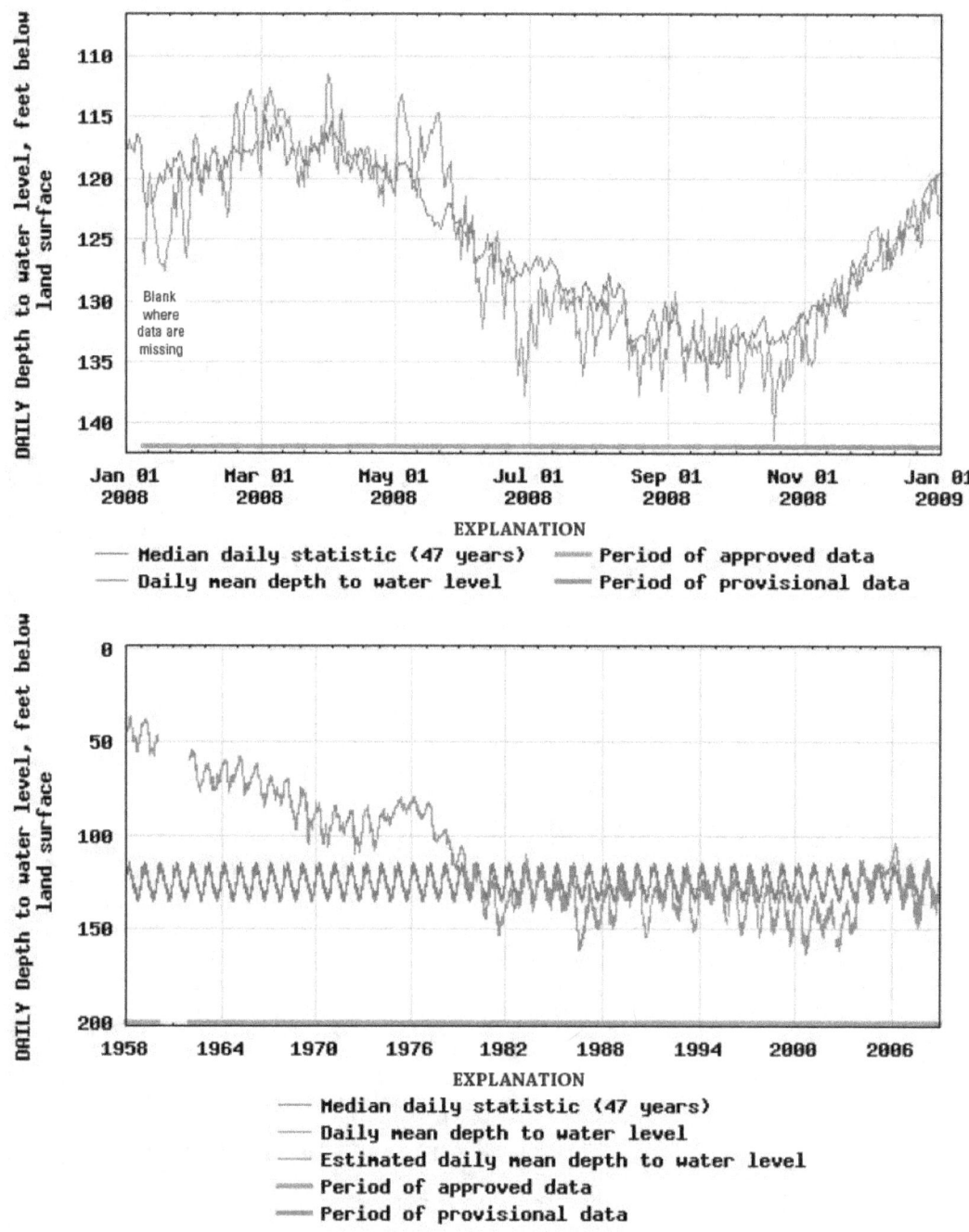

Figure A–27.   Periodic and daily mean water levels in well 13L002, Clayton aquifer, 1957–2008.

Clayton Aquifer

313105084064202   Site Name: 13L013

Latitude: 31°31'06" Longitude: 84°06'43"   Dougherty County   Period of Record: 1978 - 2008
Well Depth: 882 feet   Datum: 195 feet   Well Diameter: 60 inches

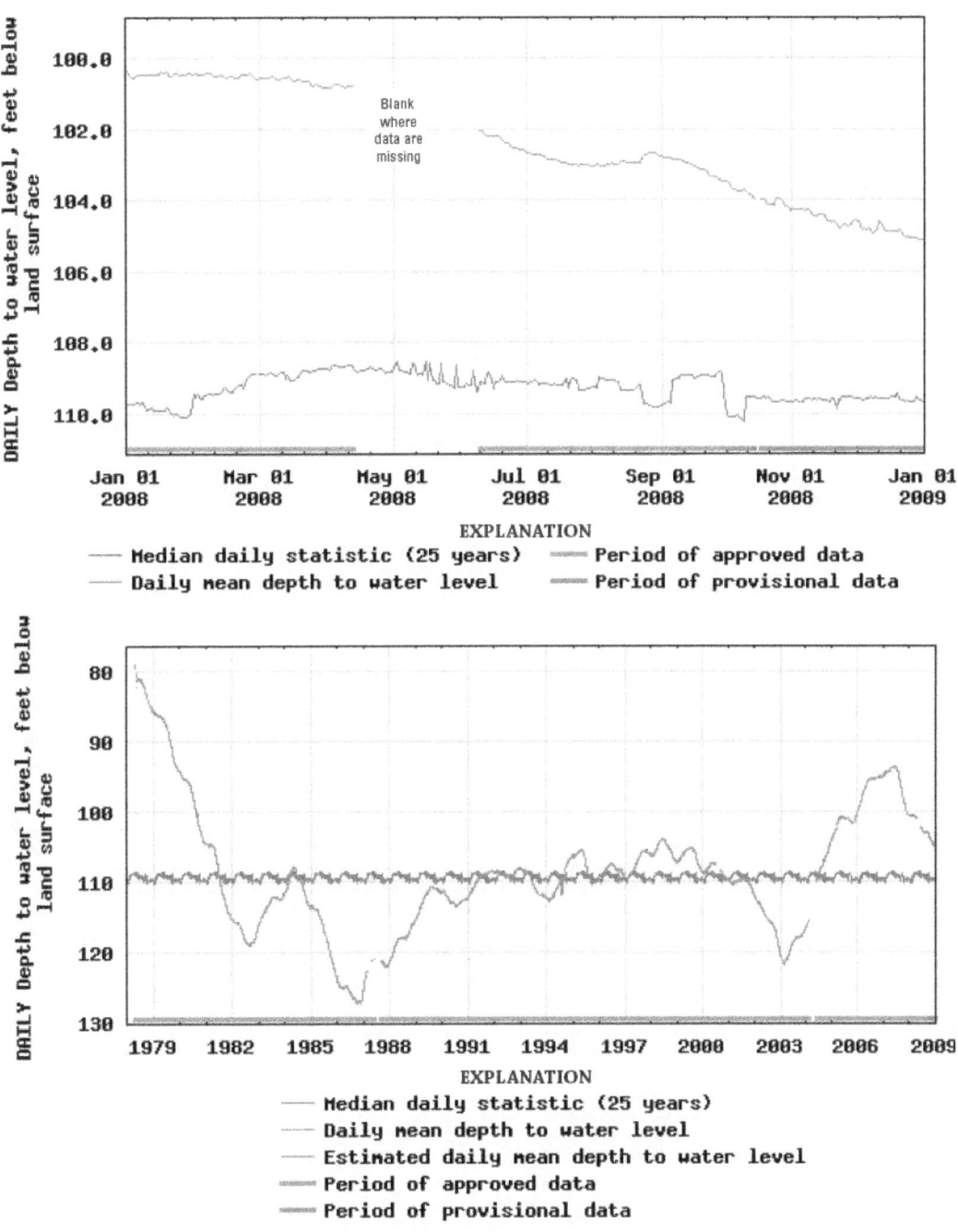

Figure A–28.   Periodic and daily mean water levels in well 13L013, Clayton aquifer, 1978–2008.

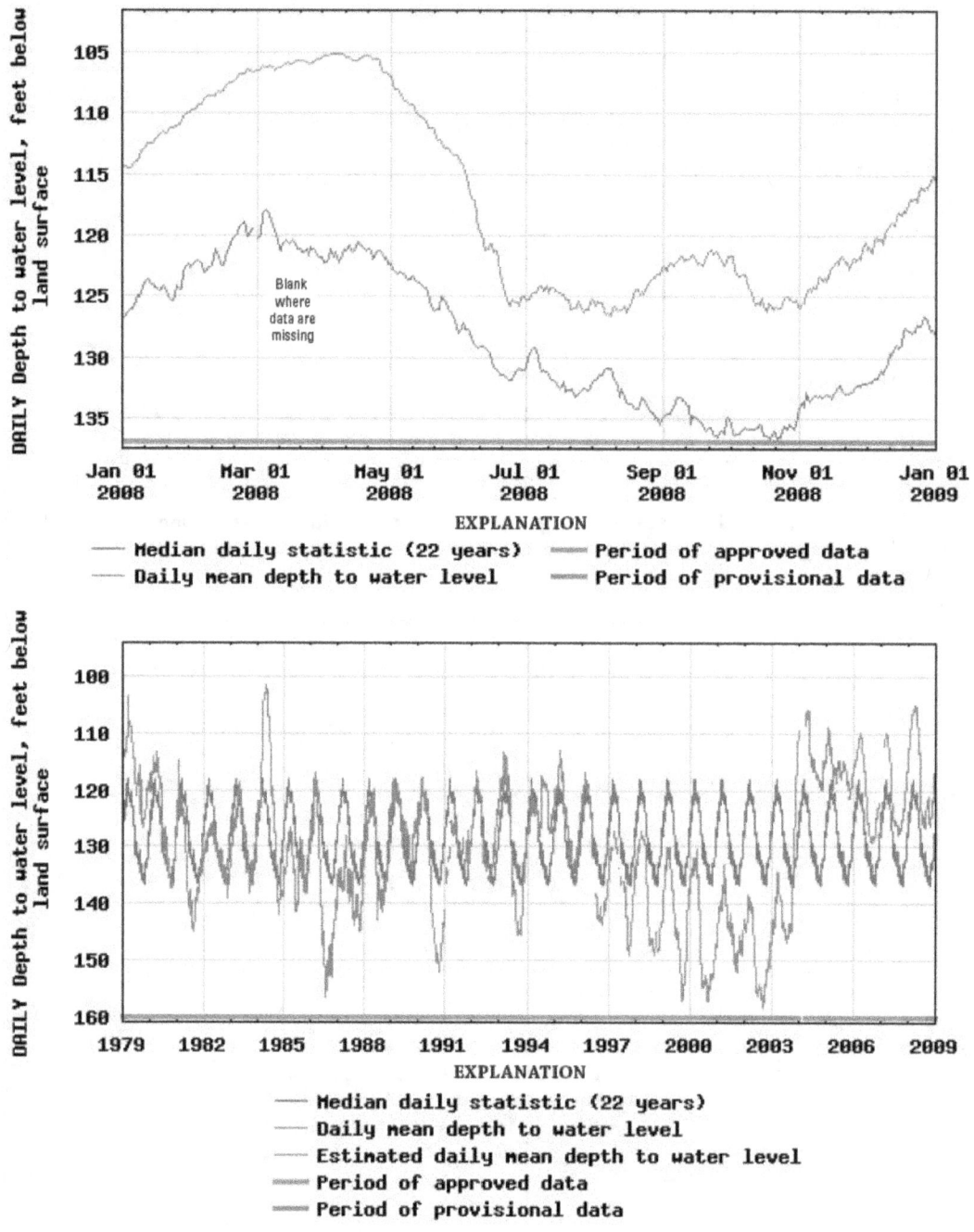

Figure A–29. Periodic and daily mean water levels in well 12L021, Cretaceous aquifer system, 1978–2008.

Appendix B.   Water-Quality Data from the Albany, Dougherty County Area, Georgia, November 2008

Table B–1. Site information for water-quality data from the Albany area of Dougherty County, Georgia, October and November 2008.

[—, no data or not applicable]

STAID Station number	SNAME Station name	DATE Date as yyyymmdd	TIME Sample start time	P72008 Depth of well, feet below land surface datum	P72019 Depth to water level, feet below land surface	P72000 Altitude of land surface, feet	P00059 Flow rate, instantaneous, gallons per minute	P72004 Pump or flow period prior to sampling, minutes
312857084132901	12K101	20081105	1325	120	51.32	205.47	—	—
312917084123001	12K129	20081105	1145	211	48.1	200	—	—
312937084131901	12K175	20081105	1540	187	44.02	198.66	—	—
312947084092201	12K180	20081104	1330	170	28.1	171.8	10	—
313020084142501	12L061	20081106	1540	195	31.36	190.15	—	—
313040084125901	12L277	20081104	1140	203	36.9	190.7	10	—
313023084113201	12L340	20081103	1730	178.5	43.47	190.82	3	—
313135084132201	12L344	20081106	1440	160	31.13	191.56	—	—
313140084130101	12L345	20081107	1000	160	36.53	196.35	—	—
313005084121401	12L348	20081106	1035	180	39.48	193	—	—
313026084121901	12L350	20081103	1545	191	35.74	189.7	3	—
313102084134301	12L357	20081106	1250	160	26.84	189.27	—	—
313000084100301	12L373	20081104	1515	170	41.35	185.9	10	—
313038084122501	12L376	20081104	1000	45	36.65	190.7	1.5	—
2352560	Flint River at GA 234, at Albany, GA	20081009	1030	—	—	150	—	—
2352560	Flint River at GA 234, at Albany, GA	20081009	1035	—	—	150	—	—
2352560	Flint River at GA 234, at Albany, GA	20081105	930	—	—	150	—	—
2352560	Flint River at GA 234, at Albany, GA	20081105	1645	—	—	150	—	—
313202084143801	12L311	20081120	1440	100	18.05	185.8	—	3
313202084143801	12L311	20081120	1020	100	18.05	185.8	—	3
313300084184901	11L020	20081118	1255	150	22.15	208	—	30
313340084220001	11L111	20081119	1230	125	25.98	220	—	2.5
313348084191601	11L077	20081118	1452	130	22	211	—	32
313440084181402	11L116	20081120	1415	150	18.76	209.86	3	50
313504084165701	11L092	20081118	1045	125	32.55	220.3	—	45
313530084203103	11L003	20081119	1650	86	15.49	220	3	46
313554084164601	11L115	20081119	1030	150	25.29	220	—	30
313604084105001	12L010	20081119	1430	895	—	193	—	15
313614084203401	11L112	20081120	1215	180	34.49	232	—	1
313650084122901	12L018	20081120	1300	830	—	231	—	5

Table B–2. Field parameters for water-quality samples from the Albany area of Dougherty County, Georgia, October and November 2008.

[C, degrees Celsius; —, no data or not applicable; <, less than; E, estimated]

STAID Station number	STAID Station numbe	P00025 Barometric pressure, millimeters of mercury	P00300 Dissolved oxygen, water, unfiltered, milligrams per liter	P00400 pH, water, unfiltered, field, standard units	P00403 pH, water, unfiltered, laboratory, standard units	P90095 Specific conductance, water, unfiltered, laboratory, microsiemens per centimeter at 25 °C	P00095 Specific conductance, water, unfiltered, microsiemens per centimeter at 25 °C	P00020 Temperature, air, °C	P00010 Temperature, water, °C
312857084132901	12K101	757	7.95	7.77	7.82	222.9	219	—	20.26
312917084123001	12K129	755	7.86	7.8	—	—	221	—	20.14
312937084131901	12K175	757	7.84	7.69	7.81	257.3	245		20.69
312947084092201	12K180	760	8.19	8	—	—	185	—	20.49
313020084142501	12L061	756	6.52	7.46	7.57	397.5	391	—	20.58
313040084125901	12L277	760	5.11	7.4	7.54	388.4	355	—	20.29
313023084113201	12L340	761	<5	7.64	—	—	282	—	21.24
313135084132201	12L344	758	0.72	7.46	7.54	333.4	332	—	20.36
313140084130101	12L345	758	3.5	7.83	7.35	338.1	322	—	20.17
313005084121401	12L348	755	7.75	7.78	7.69	336.1	335	—	20.36
313026084121901	12L350	765	—	7.16	—	—	364	—	20
313102084134301	12L357	757	1.11	7.6	7.44	393.9	393	—	20.13
313000084100301	12L373	760	7.4	7.77	—	—	263	—	20.5
313038084122501	12L376	760	6.74	7.8	7.59	380.1	384	—	20.17
2352560	Flint River at GA 234, at Albany, GA	759	7.44	6.89	7.56	128.6	132	21.5	23.14
2352560	Flint River at GA 234, at Albany, GA	759	7.44	6.89	—	—	132	21.5	23.14
2352560	Flint River at GA 234, at Albany, GA	—	—	8.49	8.08	104.4	107	—	
2352560	Flint River at GA 234, at Albany, GA	761	9.13	7.01	—	—	110	24.2	18.59
313202084143801	12L311	765	<0.5	E 7.39	—	—	293	—	E 20.85
313202084143801	12L311	765	<0.5	7.39	7.57	288.7	293	—	20.85
313300084184901	11L020	768	3.57	7.62	7.77	264.9	269	—	19.25
313340084220001	11L111	769	E 4.5	E 7.05	7.5	380.6	374	—	E 19
313348084191601	11L077	768	3.74	7.65	7.82	265	269	—	19.42
313440084181402	11L116	768	5.17	7.45	7.7	309.8	313	—	19.62
313504084165701	11L092	767	3.94	7.57	7.62	333.1	339	—	20.24
313530084203103	11L003	769	3.18	7.35	7.85	250.9	247	—	19.15
313554084164601	11L115	769	5.52	7.5	7.71	304.5	294	—	18.99
313604084105001	12L010		—	—	—	—	—	—	—
313614084203401	11L112	766	E 4	E 7.4	7.73	301.7	304		E 20
313650084122901	12L018	—	—	—	—	—	—	—	—

Table B–3.   Major cations and anions from the Albany area of Dougherty County, Georgia, October and November 2008.

[—, no data or not applicable; <, less than; E, estimated]

STAID Station number	SNAME Station name	P00915 Calcium, water, filtered	P00925 Magnesium, water, filtered	P00935 Potassium, water, filtered	P00930 Sodium, water, filtered	P00417 Acid neutralizing capacity, water, unfiltered, fixed endpoint (pH 4.5) titration, laboratory, as calcium carbonate	P90410 Acid neutralizing capacity, water, unfiltered, fixed endpoint (pH 4.5) titration, laboratory, as calcium carbonate	P00940 Chloride, water, filtered	P00950 Fluoride, water, filtered	P00955 Silica, water, filtered, as SiO$_2$	P00945 Sulfate, water, filtered
						Milligrams per liter					
312857084132901	12K101	39.33	0.495	0.309	2.101	—	95.63	4.795	<0.08	7.999	0.33
312917084123001	12K129	—	—	—	—	—	—	—	—	—	—
312937084131901	12K175	44.11	0.664	0.436	2.926		102.5	6.839	<0.08	8.198	0.253
312947084092201	12K180	—	—	—	—	—	—	—	—	—	—
313020084142501	12L061	67.29	1.645	1.069	4.511		136.5	10.619	<0.08	9.573	1.194
313040084125901	12L277	69.06	1.12	0.806	2.926	—	150.4	9.289	<0.08	9.154	1.36
313023084113201	12L340	—	—	—	—	—	—	—	—	—	—
313135084132201	12L344	62.26	0.967	0.45	2.452	—	164.6	4.492	<0.08	9.257	1.522
313140084130101	12L345	58.9	0.842	0.32	2.473		142.5	5.382	<0.08	9.39	1.049
313005084121401	12L348	58.97	1.125	0.406	3.026	—	128	9.004	<0.08	9.254	0.753
313026084121901	12L350	—	—	—	—	—	—	—	—	—	—
313102084134301	12L357	75	1.129	0.745	3.076		185.7	6.119	<0.08	9.266	3.665
313000084100301	12L373	—	—	—	—	—	—	—	—	—	—
313038084122501	12L376	66.12	1.597	1.437	2.679		139.2	10.29	E 0.044	8.815	1.623
2352560	Flint River at GA 234, at Albany, GA	—	—	—	—	45	—	—	—	—	—
2352560	Flint River at GA 234, at Albany, GA	—	—	—	—	—	—	—	—	—	—
2352560	Flint River at GA 234, at Albany, GA	7.129	1.238	1.876	9.789	—	27.94	7.264	E 0.041	9.342	9.544
313202084143801	12L311	—	—	—	—	—	—	—	—	—	—
313202084143801	12L311	56	0.473	0.6	2.285	151.2	—	3.424	E 0.04	9.057	0.447
313300084184901	11L020	53.73	0.851	0.296	1.84	137	—	3.258	E 0.063	8.964	0.551
313340084220001	11L111	81.64	0.979	0.331	1.965	206.3	—	2.645	<0.08	11.474	1.301
313348084191601	11L077	54.52	0.51	0.127	1.837	138.2	—	3.093	<0.08	7.636	0.397
313440084181402	11L116	63.81	0.591	0.179	2.49	154.5	—	5.21	<0.08	8.494	0.634
313504084165701	11L092	69.58	0.687	0.328	2.087	173.3	—	3.431	<0.08	8.72	0.475
313530084203103	11L003	49.61	0.607	0.176	1.736	130	—	3.124	<0.08	9.688	0.422
313554084164601	11L115	62.46	0.601	0.224	1.749	156	—	3.146	<0.08	8.432	0.312
313604084105001	12L010	—	—	—	—	—	—	—	—	—	—
313614084203401	11L112	61.6	1.062	0.345	2.897	154.4	—	5.012	<0.08	14.156	1.386
313650084122901	12L018	—	—	—	—	—	—	—	—	—	—

Table B–4. Nutrients and biological data from the Albany area of Dougherty County, Georgia, October and November 2008.

[C, degrees Celsius; —, no data or not applicable; <, less than; E, estimated]

STAID Station number	SNAME Station name	P00625 Ammonia plus organic nitrogen, water, unfiltered, as nitrogen	P00610 Ammonia, water, unfiltered, as nitrogen	P00631 Nitrate plus nitrite, water, filtered, as nitrogen	P00630 Nitrate plus nitrite, water, unfiltered, as nitrogen	P00613 Nitrite, water, filtered, as nitrogen	P00671 Ortho-phosphate, water, filtered, as phosphorus	P00665 Phosphorus, water, unfiltered, as phosphorus	P00680 Organic carbon, water, unfiltered	P00310 Biochemical oxygen demand, water, unfiltered, 5 days at 20 °C	P31621 Fecal coliform, A-1 broth method, 44.5 °C, 24 hours, water, most probable number per 100 milliliters
		Milligrams per liter									
312857084132901	12K101	—	—	2.946	—	0.002	—	—	—	—	—
312917084123001	12K129	—	—	3.481	—	0.002	—	—	—	—	—
312937084131901	12K175	—	—	4.969	—	0.002	—	—	—	—	—
312947084092201	12K180	—	—	2.142	—	0.002	—	—	—	—	—
313020084142501	12L061	—	—	12.506	—	0.001	—	—	—	—	—
313040084125901	12L277	—	—	8.966	—	0.002	—	—	—	—	—
313023084113201	12L340	—	—	2.677	—	0.009	—	—	—	—	—
313135084132201	12L344	—	—	1.414	—	0.002	—	—	—	—	—
313140084130101	12L345	—	—	4.464	—	0.002	—	—	—	—	—
313005084121401	12L348	—	—	7.859	—	0.002	—	—	—	—	—
313026084121901	12L350	—	—	5.249	—	0.002	—	—	—	—	—
313102084134301	12L357	—	—	2.987	—	0.002	—	—	—	—	—
313000084100301	12L373	—	—	7.964	—	0.002	—	—	—	—	—
313038084122501	12L376	—	—	10.126	—	0.002	—	—	—	—	—
2352560	Flint River at GA 234, at Albany, GA	0.31	0.06	—	0.54	—	0.02	0.18	8.15	0.75	—
2352560	Flint River at GA 234, at Albany, GA	—	—	—	—	—	—	—	—	—	500
2352560	Flint River at GA 234, at Albany, GA	—	—	0.224	—	0.003	—	—	—	—	—
313202084143801	12L311	—	—	0.04	—	<0.002	—	—	—	—	—
313300084184901	11L020	—	—	0.496	—	<0.002	—	—	—	—	—
313340084220001	11L111	—	—	0.247	—	<0.002	—	—	—	—	—
313348084191601	11L077	—	—	0.381	—	<0.002	—	—	—	—	—
313440084181402	11L116	—	—	1.593	—	<0.002	—	—	—	—	—
313504084165701	11L092	—	—	1.101	—	<0.002	—	—	—	—	—
313530084203103	11L003	—	—	0.559	—	E 0.001	—	—	—	—	—
313554084164601	11L115	—	—	1.054	—	<0.002	—	—	—	—	—
313604084105001	12L010	—	—	—	—	—	—	—	—	—	—
313614084203401	11L112	—	—	0.533	—	<0.002	—	—	—	—	—
313650084122901	12L018	—	—	—	—	—	—	—	—	—	—

Manuscript approved on October 26, 2009

For more information about this publication contact:
  USGS Georgia Water Science Center
  3039 Amwiler Road
  Atlanta, GA 30360
  telephone: 770-903-9100

  http://ga.water.usgs.gov/

Edited by Kimberly A. Waltenbaugh
Graphics and layout by Caryl J. Wipperfurth